AF687438

Also by Eric Agyemang Duah:

Perfect Prompting

The AI Uprising

The AI Messiah

The Memory Traders

Sworn Not To Love Again

MASTERING AI *In* LAW

A Practical Guide for Legal Professionals

Eric Agyemang Duah

PromptTech
Consulting
and Publishing Services

While every precaution has been taken in the preparation of this book, the publisher and author assume no responsibility for errors or omissions, or for damages resulting from the use of the information contained herein. This publication is intended for informational purposes only and does not constitute legal, professional, or technical advice. Readers are encouraged to consult qualified professionals before applying any strategies or recommendations in this book.

Mastering AI in Law: A Practical Guide for Legal Professionals

First published 2025

© 2025 Eric Agyemang Duah
All rights reserved.
No part of this publication may be reproduced, distributed, or transmitted in any form or by any means, including photocopying, recording, or other electronic or mechanical methods, without the prior written permission of the publisher.

Generative AI tools were used in the research, language refinement, and editorial review of this manuscript. All substantive analysis, interpretations, and conclusions are the sole responsibility of the author.

ISBN: 979-8230-71461-3

PromptTech Consulting and Publishing Services

To Adom Nyame,
for granting me the wisdom, knowledge, and understanding
to write this book—
a work that has become a blessing to many.

"For the Lord gives wisdom; from his mouth come knowledge and understanding."
—Proverbs 2:6 (NIV)

CONTENTS

Preface

Artificial intelligence (AI) has evolved from a theoretical concept into a transformative force reshaping the global legal landscape. The convergence of data science, natural language processing, and legal analytics is revolutionizing how lawyers conduct research, draft documents, manage compliance, and engage with clients. *Mastering AI in Law: A Practical Guide for Legal Professionals* was created to bridge the gap between AI's technological potential and its practical application in legal practice.

This guide connects legal theory with digital practice through structured, real-world exercises and prompt engineering techniques—the art and science of designing precise inputs to optimize AI responses. It demonstrates how to leverage a dual-layered ecosystem: foundational models such as ChatGPT, Gemini, and Microsoft Copilot for general productivity, alongside specialized AI-powered legal platforms like Lexis+ AI, Harvey AI, CoCounsel, and Clio, which support high-stakes, jurisdiction-specific workflows.

Significant emphasis has been placed on the ethical, regulatory, and professional dimensions of AI use. Topics such as confidentiality, bias, accountability, and data protection are woven throughout to ensure readers not only know how to use AI systems but understand how to do so responsibly within legal and ethical boundaries.

To provide a logical learning path, this book is organized into six parts:

- Part I introduces the conceptual foundations and regulatory landscape surrounding AI in law.
- Part II offers a framework for selecting and integrating appropriate tools, from open models to enterprise legal suites.
- Parts III and IV deliver core technical training, focusing on prompt engineering to maximize AI performance for specific legal tasks.
- Part V addresses the vital need for verification by outlining protocols to detect AI hallucinations and mitigate bias.
- Part VI serves as a toolkit, presenting curated "Prompt Packs" for immediate application across various legal specialties.

As the legal profession enters an era of AI-augmented practice, mastery of prompt design, tool selection, and ethical reasoning will distinguish the capable from the complacent. This book serves both as a practical reference and a strategic roadmap for legal professionals dedicated to advancing the profession responsibly through technological innovation.

——— Eric Agyemang Duah

Introduction

The legal profession stands at a turning point. For decades, technology has played a supportive role—automating billing, managing documents, and streamlining communication. Today, the rise of Generative Artificial Intelligence (GenAI) marks a profound shift, transforming technology from a mere utility into a cognitive partner. The ability to generate, summarize, and critique legal text instantly demands a fundamental reassessment of the legal professional's core toolkit.

Mastering AI in Law: A Practical Guide for Legal Professionals addresses this rapid evolution head-on. It begins with the premise that AI competence is no longer optional—it is now a central element of the professional duty of diligence. The legal landscape is divided between two groups: those who harness AI to amplify their expertise, and those who risk being left behind. This book is designed to help readers join the former.

The primary goal is to provide a comprehensive, practical manual for safely and effectively integrating AI across all areas of legal practice. Moving beyond abstract discussions about "the future of law," this guide focuses on actionable skills that legal professionals need today.

The immediate challenge is not merely access to AI tools but mastering the entire process from crafting precise prompts to verifying outputs. Tools like ChatGPT,

Gemini, and Lexis+ AI are powerful but carry risks—including hallucinations, which are fabricated or inaccurate outputs, and algorithmic bias. Using these tools without a reliable verification method can create ethical and professional liabilities.

The Solution: A Practical, Process-Driven Methodology

This book offers a structured methodology designed to transform artificial intelligence from a potential liability into a controlled professional asset. It equips legal professionals with both the technical skills and governance frameworks necessary to mitigate risk while maximizing value.

By the end of this guide, readers will be able to:

- Define and mitigate risks by understanding the regulatory environment governing AI use, including the General Data Protection Regulation, the California Consumer Privacy Act, and the Children's Online Privacy Protection Act, alongside applicable professional and ethical standards.
- Master the input layer by crafting precise, context-rich prompts that consistently produce accurate, relevant, and legally useful outputs.
- Verify outputs using structured protocols designed to detect hallucination, surface bias, and ensure factual and legal reliability.
- Maximize return on investment by strategically deploying AI tools to enhance efficiency in legal research, drafting, analysis, and client communication, thereby strengthening competitive advantage without compromising professional standards.

How to Use This Guide: A Six-Part Roadmap

To support progressive learning and practical adoption, this book is organized into six interrelated parts, each building on the previous one:

- **Part I: Foundations of AI in Law**
  Introduces the fundamental technologies underpinning artificial intelligence, addresses common misconceptions, and examines the ethical and professional responsibilities associated with AI use in legal practice.

- **Part II: AI Tools and Their Integration**
  Translates theory into practice by offering a framework for evaluating, selecting, and integrating AI tools—ranging from general-purpose models to specialized legal platforms such as Harvey AI, CoCounsel, and Clio.

- **Part III: Mastering Legal Prompt Engineering**
  Focuses on the foundational skill that governs AI performance: prompt engineering. This part explores advanced techniques such as role assignment, negative prompting, constraint setting, and iterative refinement.

- **Part IV: Crafting Effective Prompts for Legal Tasks**
  Applies prompt engineering principles to high-value legal workflows, including contract drafting, litigation preparation, statutory interpretation, and regulatory analysis.

- **Part V: Evaluating and Refining AI Outputs**
  Emphasizes verification as a professional obligation, presenting protocols for auditing AI-generated content, preventing hallucinations, mitigating bias, and safeguarding confidentiality.

- **Part VI: Prompt Packs for Legal Specialties**
  Serves as an applied toolkit, providing customizable prompt templates and workflows designed for immediate use across diverse legal practice areas.

Mastering AI in Law is not a survey of legal technology trends. It is a professional handbook for operating competently and ethically in an AI-augmented legal environment. Its guiding commitment is clear: technological advancement must reinforce, not erode, the core legal values of diligence, integrity, accuracy, and justice.

Part I

Foundations of AI in Law

Understanding AI in Legal Practice

The legal profession, rooted in tradition and meticulous processes, is experiencing a profound transformation driven by the rise of artificial intelligence (AI). Far beyond simple automation, AI revolutionizes how legal professionals work by providing tools that enhance efficiency, deepen insights, and elevate client service.

AI enables lawyers to conduct legal research, draft documents, analyze cases, and develop litigation strategies with unprecedented speed and accuracy. By automating repetitive and high-volume tasks, it frees legal professionals to focus on high-value activities such as strategic planning, complex problem-solving, and client advocacy.

This chapter establishes the foundational understanding of AI's role in legal workflows, beginning with the fundamental question: What is artificial intelligence? Through a detailed exploration of its definition, underlying mechanisms, and diverse applications, this chapter equips readers with insight into the transformative potential of AI, particularly within the legal domain.

Defining Artificial Intelligence

Artificial intelligence, or AI, is a dynamic and evolving field that expands the computational capabilities of modern systems. Fundamentally, AI involves the creation of algorithms and systems capable of performing tasks that traditionally require human intelligence, such as learning, problem-solving, and decision-making.

A Foundational Definition

John McCarthy, regarded as the "father of AI" for coining the term *(Artificial Intelligence)* and organizing the 1956 Dartmouth Conference, provided a seminal definition in the original 1955 conference proposal. He described AI as *"the science and engineering of making intelligent machines"* (McCarthy et al., 1955). This definition was based on the conjecture that every aspect of learning, or any other feature of intelligence, can in principle be so precisely described that a machine can be made to simulate it.

This captures the core ambition of AI, which is to replicate human-like cognitive functions through precise, programmable means. Unlike traditional software, which executes fixed instructions based on rigid logic, AI systems are designed to adapt, learn from experience, and operate with a degree of autonomy to achieve specific goals. For the legal professional, this distinction is critical, as it marks the shift from technology that merely stores data to technology that can assist in the reasoning and analysis of that data.

AI vs. Traditional Rule-Based Software

To fully appreciate the transformative power of AI, it is essential to distinguish it from the rule-based software that has supported the legal profession for decades. Traditional software, including practice management and legacy document systems, is deterministic, operating strictly on fixed, predefined rules, often described by the logic of "If X, then Y." While effective at managing structured data, traditional software cannot adapt without manual reprogramming, and it typically automates rigid, repetitive processes.

In sharp contrast, AI systems are probabilistic, leveraging advanced mathematical models to identify patterns across vast and varied datasets to make informed predictions. AI excels at processing unstructured data, such as contracts, case files, and emails, and it continuously adapts as it ingests new information. Crucially, whereas traditional software outputs fixed, predictable results, AI generates variable, novel outputs, such as drafting a tailored contract clause or summarizing a complex legal argument.

This distinction means AI does not simply automate routine tasks, it augments human cognition by managing complexity and ambiguity, thereby freeing legal professionals to concentrate on strategic analysis and client-facing work. To understand how this augmentation works in practice, the next chapter explores the core technologies driving these AI capabilities.

2

Core Components of AI

Having established a foundational understanding of artificial intelligence and its distinction from traditional, rule-based software, this chapter examines the core technologies powering modern legal applications.

The field of AI encompasses several interrelated domains, with machine learning and natural language processing serving as the foundational components for modern legal work. Specialized capabilities, such as generative AI, computer vision, and robotic process automation, extend these foundations for targeted uses, including content creation, visual evidence analysis, and workflow automation.

1. Machine Learning (ML)

Machine learning is a cornerstone of AI, enabling systems to learn from data and improve their performance over time without explicit, manual programming. Within the legal field, machine learning transforms raw data into actionable intelligence through three primary applications: predictive analytics, fraud detection, and document classification.

In the realm of predictive analytics, machine learning leverages vast amounts of historical case data to forecast potential outcomes. Lawyers utilize these models to gauge the success rate of a case based on variables such as jurisdiction, case type, and past judicial decisions, which allows for rigorous, data-driven risk assessment. Beyond prediction, machine learning algorithms are critical for fraud detection and compliance monitoring.

By examining financial records and contracts, these systems identify anomalies, such as unusual patterns in financial statements, that might indicate corporate malfeasance. Finally, machine learning brings order to the massive volume of information firms handle through document classification. In e-Discovery, for instance, machine learning systems automate the sorting process, rapidly categorizing millions of files as privileged, evidence, or correspondence based on their specific content and context.

2. Natural Language Processing (NLP)

Natural language processing enables AI to understand, interpret, and generate human language. As the law is fundamentally a language-based profession, natural language processing is essential to legal AI, driving efficiency in contract analysis, legal research, and document summarization.

NLP-powered tools revolutionize contract analysis by automatically extracting critical clauses, such as payment terms, liability limits, and termination conditions. These systems can flag ambiguous language or provisions that may lead to future disputes, providing lawyers with the insights needed for precise drafting. This linguistic capability extends to legal research, where AI-powered platforms process complex queries to retrieve relevant case precedents and statutory references without relying on rigid keyword searches. Furthermore,

NLP algorithms excel at document summarization, distilling lengthy court opinions or memoranda into concise overviews, which allows professionals to absorb key decisions without being overwhelmed by a high volume of text.

3. Generative AI (GenAI) and Large Language Models (LLMs)

Generative AI represents a technological leap focused on creating entirely new content rather than merely classifying existing data. Large Language Models, or LLMs, such as those powering ChatGPT, Gemini, and specialized legal platforms like Harvey or CoCounsel, are a specific class of generative AI trained on vast datasets of text.

Unlike traditional tools that only analyze text, LLMs are designed to generate it, facilitating novel content creation. Building on the foundations of machine learning and natural language processing, this capability allows lawyers to draft pleadings, create client communications, or outline complex legal arguments in a fraction of the time traditionally required. These models leverage a deep statistical understanding of syntax and semantics to maintain contextual coherence, producing legally relevant text that adheres to professional stylistic norms. However, the utility of generative AI is entirely dependent on prompt-based interaction. The quality and accuracy of the output are directly tied to the precision of the user's input, making "prompt engineering" a vital skill for the modern practitioner.

4. Computer Vision

Computer vision enables machines to interpret and understand visual data, a capability that is becoming increasingly valuable for evidence handling and the digitization of physical records.

In litigation, visual evidence analysis tools can enhance the clarity of surveillance footage or detect alterations in images, which helps to verify authenticity in fraud or criminal cases. This technology also powers advanced document analysis through Optical Character Recognition, or OCR. By combining OCR with vision algorithms, AI systems can extract text from scanned PDFs or handwritten notes, converting them into editable, searchable formats. Additionally, computer vision supports security protocols through facial recognition and biometric identity verification, which are increasingly used within law firms and court systems to restrict access to sensitive environments.

5. Robotics and RPA

Robotics integrates mechanical or software systems with AI to bridge the gap between digital intelligence and physical or administrative execution. In the legal sector, this integration manifests in both digital and physical forms.

The most prevalent application is Robotic Process Automation, or RPA, which utilizes "software bots" to automate repetitive digital tasks. RPA systems streamline administrative workflows, such as document filing, scheduling, and compliance reporting, while significantly minimizing human error. On the physical front, specialized applications are emerging to enhance access to justice. For example, robotic kiosks designed to provide basic legal information to self-represented litigants are being deployed in several jurisdictions to assist with wayfinding and procedural guidance. While these physical systems significantly improve access to justice for underserved populations, they simultaneously introduce complex regulatory challenges regarding professional liability and the unauthorized practice of law.

3

Misconceptions About AI in Legal Work

Despite the immense potential AI offers for transforming the legal profession, its adoption is often hindered by skepticism and persistent myths. Many legal professionals, particularly those less familiar with the technology's current capabilities, harbor reservations about its practical application. This section addresses these common misconceptions, clarifying how AI functions not as a replacement, but as an essential asset in modern legal practice.

The Myth of Lawyer Replacement

Perhaps the most pervasive misconception is the fear that AI will replace lawyers. This belief stems from the assumption that AI's data analysis capabilities render human judgment obsolete. However, this view fundamentally misunderstands the design of legal AI. These systems are built to augment, not replace, the legal professional. By automating time-consuming, repetitive tasks—such as document review, initial contract analysis, and discovery sorting—AI provides data-driven insights that free lawyers to focus on what machines cannot do: strategic planning, complex negotiation, and high-level client advocacy. In this sense, AI acts as a sophisticated force multiplier, empowering lawyers to deliver higher-quality services more efficiently.

The "Complexity" Barrier

Another common barrier is the belief that AI is too complex for practical integration, requiring advanced technical skills or a background in data science. In reality, modern legal AI tools are increasingly democratized. Platforms like CoCounsel, Lexis+ AI, and ChatGPT utilize Natural Language Processing (NLP) to understand plain English queries. A lawyer need not write code; they simply need to ask a question as they would to a junior associate. These intuitive interfaces allow practitioners to leverage powerful computing without a steep learning curve, making the technology accessible to tech-savvy and traditional lawyers alike.

Addressing the "Nuance" Gap

Critics often argue that AI lacks the capacity to grasp the subtlety of legal reasoning or the context of a specific case. While it is true that AI cannot currently replicate the depth of human wisdom or moral judgment, the misconception lies in discarding the tool because of this limitation. AI's role is to provide the foundational analysis—identifying patterns across millions of documents or citing relevant case law—which creates a solid baseline for the lawyer to apply their specific expertise. The AI handles the volume; the lawyer handles the nuance. By integrating AI, legal professionals gain a data-driven foundation that supports, rather than supplants, their professional judgment.

Security and Ethical Standards

Security concerns, particularly regarding client confidentiality and data privacy, frequently deter adoption. While these are valid concerns, the misconception is that *all* AI tools are insecure. Enterprise-grade legal AI solutions are built to adhere to rigorous standards, including SOC 2 compliance and zero-retention policies (where the AI does not retain, or train on client's data). Leading platforms employ robust encryption and data "fencing" to safeguard sensitive information. Furthermore, the industry is actively addressing ethical risks, such as algorithmic bias, through the development of professional guidelines. By selecting reputable, compliant vendors, lawyers can mitigate these risks effectively.

The Democratization of Legal Tech

Finally, it is often assumed that AI is the exclusive domain of large law firms with substantial IT budgets. While "Big Law" may have led early adoption, the rise of Generative AI has leveled the playing field. Solutions are becoming increasingly affordable, with tools like ChatGPT Enterprise, Gemini, and Perplexity offering powerful drafting and summarization capabilities at a fraction of the cost of legacy software. This accessibility enables small and mid-sized firms to compete on efficiency and quality, delivering sophisticated legal services without the overhead previously required.

Conclusion

Addressing these misconceptions reveals AI as a collaborator rather than a competitor. By understanding the reality of the technology—that it is accessible, secure, and designed for augmentation—legal professionals can move past hesitation and embrace a future where technology and human expertise work in tandem.

4

The Benefits of AI in Legal Practice

The introduction of artificial intelligence (AI) into the legal profession has ushered in a new era defined by efficiency, heightened accuracy, and cost-effectiveness. Far from a theoretical luxury, AI tools are actively reshaping and transforming legal workflows, making practice more agile, precise, and strategically informed. This section explores how AI is revolutionizing key aspects of legal work, providing a comprehensive understanding of its critical role in the modern firm.

Enhanced Efficiency and the Shift to High-Value Work

AI-powered tools enable lawyers to automate the repetitive tasks that traditionally consumed significant time and effort. From conducting basic legal research to drafting template documents and reviewing discovery, AI can execute these processes exponentially faster than any human.

Systems utilizing Natural Language Processing (NLP), such as Contract Lifecycle Management (CLM) platforms, can read, interpret, and categorize vast amounts of legal text in minutes, generating initial drafts or flagging compliance issues based on defined parameters. By offloading this high-volume work, AI allows legal professionals to focus their capacity entirely on high-value tasks that require human judgment: client interaction, strategic planning, complex problem-solving, and courtroom advocacy. This strategic allocation of time is the core driver of modern efficiency gains.

Cost Reduction and Market Democratization

For law firms of all sizes, AI offers a compelling pathway to lowered operational costs and resource optimization. The financial burden of employing large teams of junior associates or paralegals for data-intensive work, such as sifting through millions of e-Discovery files, is substantially reduced when AI-powered tools accomplish the same task in a fraction of the time and cost.

This is especially critical for solo practitioners and smaller law firms. The cost reduction democratizes sophisticated technology, granting access to high-quality legal research and drafting support through affordable, yet robust, platforms like ChatGPT Enterprise, Gemini, or specialized legal systems like CoCounsel. By integrating these solutions, smaller firms can compete effectively by enhancing productivity, reducing overhead, and delivering high-quality, cost-effective services previously exclusive to large, resource-rich firms.

Superior Research and Data-Driven Strategy

One of AI's most profound benefits is its ability to conduct in-depth legal research at unprecedented speed and precision. AI-powered tools, such as Lexis+ AI and CoCounsel, use advanced algorithms to analyze massive volumes of case law, statutes, and commentary.

Legal research that once took days can now be completed in minutes, providing lawyers with relevant precedents and insights tailored to a specific query. This speed provides a significant competitive edge, allowing attorneys to swiftly shape arguments and adapt strategies. Furthermore, predictive analytics, powered by Machine Learning, goes beyond simple retrieval to forecast potential case outcomes based on past judicial behavior and data trends. This capability enables lawyers to provide clients with strategic, data-informed advice on whether to pursue litigation or settlement.

Improved Accuracy and Error Mitigation

Given the high stakes of legal work, the precision of legal documents and filings is paramount. AI systems offer a distinct advantage over human review regarding precision and consistency.

Through Document Review AI and specialized Contract Analysis Software, these tools can automatically scan, flag, and correct errors in legal documents, identifying inconsistencies, missing critical clauses, or incorrect legal references. AI can perform real-time compliance checks against a predefined set of laws and regulations, significantly reducing the risk of costly human oversight. This process minimizes the likelihood of expensive mistakes or malpractice claims, ensuring that the final work product is accurate, compliant, and defensible.

Elevated Client Experience and Fostering Innovation

AI is not just an internal tool; it is a means to elevate the client experience and drive long-term innovation. Many firms now integrate AI-powered chatbots to handle initial client intake, offer transparent case status updates, and streamline appointment scheduling, making legal interaction more accessible and less administrative.

By allowing lawyers to focus on personalized consultation, AI helps create tailored legal solutions that align with individual client needs and goals, thereby improving satisfaction and increasing referrals. Looking ahead, this technological foundation enables practices to become future-ready, paving the way for innovations like smart contracts—self-executing agreements that automatically enforce terms without intermediaries—and new service models that attract a generation of tech-savvy clients.

Conclusion

The benefits of AI in legal practice are vast and multifaceted. Whether improving efficiency, reducing costs, enhancing research capabilities, increasing accuracy, or driving innovation, AI has the potential to fundamentally revolutionize the legal profession. For law firms of all sizes, embracing AI is not merely about staying competitive—it is about future-proofing their practice. The firms that effectively integrate AI tools into their workflows will be the ones that can deliver the highest quality service at the most competitive rate, benefiting both themselves and their clients in the long run.

5

Legal AI Regulations and Compliance

The integration of artificial intelligence into legal practice requires operation within a complex and rapidly evolving regulatory environment. Legal AI tools, including systems used for research, document analysis, risk assessment, and predictive analytics, are increasingly subject to legal, ethical, and professional oversight. Although only a limited number of jurisdictions have enacted AI-specific statutes, regulatory obligations governing legal AI arise through a layered framework of data protection laws, sector-specific regulations, professional conduct rules, and national or supranational AI governance instruments.

This chapter examines the global regulatory landscape governing legal AI, emphasizing compliance obligations, ethical foundations, and jurisdiction-specific requirements that shape the responsible deployment of artificial intelligence in legal settings.

Global Standards and Ethical Foundations

International institutions have established foundational frameworks that guide artificial intelligence governance worldwide, creating a shared ethical baseline for deployment across sectors, including the legal profession.

The Organisation for Economic Co-operation and Development (OECD) Principles on Artificial Intelligence (2019) articulate core expectations for trustworthy AI, including transparency, accountability, robustness, security, and respect for human rights. Although non-binding, these principles function as an influential reference point for national legislation, regulatory coordination, and cross-border interoperability.

Building on this foundation, the United Nations Educational, Scientific and Cultural Organization (UNESCO) Recommendation on the Ethics of Artificial Intelligence (2021) places particular emphasis on inclusivity, human dignity, and the mitigation of structural bias. In legal contexts, these principles underscore the necessity of human oversight, procedural fairness, non-discriminatory outcomes, and safeguards for due process when artificial intelligence is used in judicial or quasi-judicial functions.

Together, these instruments establish a global expectation that legal AI systems must remain explainable, accountable, and subordinate to human decision-making authority.

Jurisdictional Regulations

The European Union

The European Union currently leads global artificial intelligence regulation through the Artificial Intelligence Act, which entered into force in August 1, 2024. The Act adopts a tiered, risk-based regulatory model that categorizes artificial intelligence systems based on their potential impact on fundamental rights and public interests.

Prohibitions on unacceptable-risk systems and obligations relating to artificial intelligence literacy began applying on February 2, 2025. Governance obligations for providers of General Purpose AI (GPAI) models apply from August 2, 2025. Legal artificial intelligence systems classified as high-risk, including those used for judicial analytics, legal decision support, or access-to-justice applications, must comply with stringent requirements related to data governance, record-keeping, transparency, and human oversight. Full applicability for most high-risk legal systems is phased for August 2026 and beyond.

Complementing the AI Act is the General Data Protection Regulation (GDPR), which governs the processing of personal data in artificial intelligence systems. Article 22, addressing automated decision-making with legal or similarly significant effects, is particularly relevant for legal AI tools used in litigation analytics, client profiling, or risk scoring. These systems must ensure meaningful human review and procedural safeguards.

The European Union is further strengthening its framework through proposals such as the AI Liability Directive, which seeks to modernize civil liability rules for harm caused by artificial intelligence systems.

The United States

The United States employs a sector-specific, decentralized model, lacking a single federal AI statute. The compliance landscape is instead a combination of non-binding federal guidance and a growing patchwork of state laws.

At the federal level, the National Institute of Standards and Technology (NIST) has issued the AI Risk Management Framework (AI RMF), which serves as the primary governance standard for risk identification, mitigation, and accountability across industries, including legal services.

Federal policy has recently shifted toward deregulation, reflected in Executive Order 14179 (January 2025), which emphasizes innovation and revokes prior executive restrictions on AI development. As a result, binding AI compliance obligations increasingly emerge at the state level.

States such as California continue to lead, through the California Consumer Privacy Act (CCPA) and emerging AI transparency legislation affecting large-scale model developers. Other states, including Colorado and Utah, now require disclosures when consumers interact with generative artificial intelligence systems, creating a fragmented and evolving compliance landscape.

AI regulation in the United States also intersects with child data protections under the Children's Online Privacy Protection Act (COPPA), which imposes strict consent and data minimization requirements when systems process information relating to children under thirteen. Legal AI tools used in family law, education advocacy, or juvenile justice must carefully comply with these obligations.

Other Major Jurisdictions

Canada

Canada's AI governance framework emphasizes accountability and transparency. The Directive on Automated Decision-Making applies to federal institutions and imposes detailed requirements for algorithmic impact assessments and explainability.

While the Artificial Intelligence and Data Act (AIDA), introduced as part of Bill C-27, remains under consideration without enactment as of December 2025, commercial legal AI deployments remain primarily governed by the Personal Information Protection and Electronic Documents Act (PIPEDA), which regulates the collection, use, and disclosure of personal data in private-sector activities.

The United Kingdom

The United Kingdom adopts a pro-innovation, regulator-led approach grounded in the Data Protection Act 2018 and United Kingdom General Data Protection Regulation. Rather than enacting a single AI statute, sector regulators, including the Information Commissioner's Office, issue guidance on applying existing principles of fairness, accountability, and transparency to artificial intelligence.

For legal practitioners, this approach requires transparency regarding AI use, documentation of decision logic, and human oversight where AI influences client-facing or case-related outcomes.

Asia-Pacific: Singapore, Australia, and Japan

The Asia-Pacific region presents a diverse regulatory landscape, blending voluntary frameworks with emerging mandatory standards.

Singapore

A global leader in practical governance, Singapore relies on its Model AI Governance Framework. This voluntary guide emphasizes explainability and fairness, providing granular detail for private sector implementation. For legal AI, Singapore's focus on "human-centric" AI ensures that client advisory tools remain transparent and accountable.

Australia

Australia is transitioning from a voluntary AI Ethics Framework toward mandatory guardrails for high-risk settings. Legal AI tools used in Australia must also comply with the Privacy Act 1988, which dictates obligations regarding consent and the secure processing of personal information.

Japan

Japan adopts an "innovation-first" approach through its Social Principles of Human-Centric AI. The governance landscape is shaped by the AI Guidelines for Business, which encourage voluntary corporate initiatives regarding fairness and privacy. However, recent moves suggest a tightening of regulations specifically regarding copyright and the protection of creative data used to train AI models.

The Middle East

Middle Eastern jurisdictions are increasingly formalizing AI governance through a combination of national strategies, ethical frameworks, and data protection legislation. While comprehensive AI statutes remain limited, regulatory oversight is expanding rapidly, particularly in high-impact sectors such as law and finance.

United Arab Emirates

The UAE applies the UAE AI Charter alongside the Personal Data Protection Law (Federal Decree-Law No. 45 of 2021). While the AI Charter functions as a policy framework, the data protection law imposes binding obligations regarding automated decision-making and personal data processing. Financial and legal free zones, such as the Dubai International Financial Centre, maintain additional regulatory controls.

Saudi Arabia

Saudi Arabia's AI governance is led by the Saudi Data and Artificial Intelligence Authority (SDAIA), which has issued a national Artificial Intelligence Ethics Framework. Although this framework operates primarily as guidance, it is reinforced by binding obligations under the Personal Data Protection Law, including localization requirements for sensitive data. Legal decision-making systems are generally treated as high-risk applications, requiring enhanced scrutiny, risk assessments, and human oversight.

Qatar

Qatar regulates AI use in legal and financial institutions primarily through sectoral oversight. The Qatar Central Bank has issued binding regulatory guidance requiring financial institutions to maintain governance, transparency, and accountability for automated systems, including those used for legal risk assessment and compliance functions. These measures align with international standards, even in the absence of a standalone AI statute.

South America

South American jurisdictions are increasingly adopting rights-centered approaches to AI governance, emphasizing transparency, accountability, and individual remedies.

Brazil

Brazil's proposed Legal Framework for Artificial Intelligence (PL 2338/2023) represents the region's most advanced legislative initiative. Although not yet enacted, the framework adopts a risk-based classification system and establishes rights to explanation and contestation for decisions generated by automated systems, particularly in employment, credit, and consumer contexts. Until enactment, AI compliance in legal practice is governed primarily by Brazil's data protection regime and consumer protection laws.

Argentina

In Argentina, judicial and administrative initiatives have advanced AI governance ahead of comprehensive legislation. Under the Personal Data Protection Act (Law No. 25.326), regulators increasingly emphasize transparency and accountability for automated processing. Courts and public institutions have begun requiring disclosures when AI systems are used, signaling a trend toward heightened liability standards for AI-related harm.

Across the region, there is a growing trend toward strict liability for artificial intelligence-related harm, placing heightened responsibility on deployers of legal technology.

Africa

African approaches to AI regulation balance economic development objectives with strong concerns around data sovereignty, fairness, and human rights protection.

At the continental level, the African Union Artificial Intelligence Strategy encourages member states to prioritize data localization, linguistic diversity, and cultural relevance. While not legally binding, the strategy aligns AI governance with the African Charter on Human and Peoples' Rights, influencing domestic regulatory approaches.

Nigeria

Nigeria regulates AI primarily through the Nigeria Data Protection Act (NDPA), which imposes restrictions on cross-border data transfers and mandates lawful processing of personal data used in AI systems. Innovation is supported by the

National Centre for Artificial Intelligence and Robotics (NCAIR), which operates within a framework emphasizing national data sovereignty.

South Africa

In South Africa, the Protection of Personal Information Act (POPIA) governs automated decision-making, particularly under Section 71, which regulates decisions that have legal or similarly significant effects on individuals. The Information Regulator has increasingly scrutinized AI-enabled systems used in legal, employment, and financial contexts.

Egypt

Egypt has positioned itself as a regional leader in legal technology through its National Artificial Intelligence Strategy (2025–2030). Although the strategy is policy-driven rather than statutory, AI deployment is governed by Law No. 151 of 2020 (Personal Data Protection Law). Judicial initiatives, including "Smart Justice" programs, integrate AI into court administration and online dispute resolution while expressly maintaining that AI must not replace the discretionary reasoning of judges.

Practical Implications for Africa

For legal practitioners, these frameworks create heightened obligations around data localization, bias mitigation, and transparency. AI models trained on foreign datasets may require additional validation to ensure linguistic, biometric, and cultural accuracy before deployment in African legal contexts.

Key Considerations for Implementation and Professional Duty

While statutory and regulatory compliance provides a baseline, responsible AI deployment in legal practice extends beyond formal legal requirements. Professional duty demands that lawyers integrate ethical safeguards, technical reliability standards, and governance controls into every stage of AI adoption.

Accordingly, the following considerations represent the operational pillars through which legal professionals can translate regulatory principles into defensible, ethical, and client-centered AI practice:

1. **Data Privacy & Security:** Safeguarding client data remains paramount. Legal AI tools must comply with applicable data protection regimes and implement robust technical safeguards, including encryption, access controls, and clear data retention policies.

2. **Algorithmic Auditing and Bias Mitigation:** Regular audits are essential to detect and mitigate bias, inaccuracies, or discriminatory outputs. Firms should document training data sources, testing methodologies, and corrective measures to ensure accountability.

3. **Transparency and Explainability:** Transparency strengthens client confidence. Firms should communicate clearly about the role of AI in legal service delivery, including its capabilities, limitations, and the reasoning behind outputs. Explainability is critical when AI tools are used in matters involving vulnerable populations, where regulations often mandate clear disclosures.

4. **Human Oversight and Professional Judgment:** AI must always enhance, but never substitute, professional legal judgment. Firms must establish clear governance structures and quality-control mechanisms that mandate continuous human oversight. This ensures that AI systems align with both ethical standards and the practitioner's ultimate responsibility to the client, effectively mitigating the risks associated with automated decision-making.

Conclusion

Legal AI operates within a layered and rapidly evolving regulatory environment. Understanding global standards, jurisdiction-specific laws, and professional obligations is essential for ethical and compliant legal practice. As artificial intelligence governance continues to mature, regulatory frameworks will expand, enforcement mechanisms will sharpen, and judicial interpretations will further refine the boundaries of permissible use.

Accordingly, legal professionals must treat regulatory awareness as an ongoing responsibility rather than a one-time exercise. Practitioners deploying artificial intelligence systems should regularly monitor legislative updates, regulatory guidance, and enforcement trends within their relevant jurisdictions to ensure continued compliance and professional competence.

Through disciplined governance, sustained human oversight, and a commitment to responsible innovation, legal professionals can harness the benefits of artificial intelligence while safeguarding fairness, accountability, and the integrity of the legal process.

Part II

AI Tools and Their Integration

Key AI Tools for Legal Work

The legal profession is undergoing a structural transformation driven by the integration of Artificial Intelligence (AI) into core legal workflows. From legal research and drafting to client communication, matter management, and predictive analysis, AI tools are redefining how legal professionals process information, manage complexity, and deliver value.

This chapter examines some key AI technologies currently shaping legal practice. To assist practitioners in navigating an increasingly crowded and fragmented marketplace, the tools are grouped into two categories: General-Purpose Large Language Models (LLMs) and Specialized Legal AI Platforms. Each tool is assessed based on its functional capabilities, pricing structure, accessibility, security posture, and global applicability, enabling informed decisions regarding adoption and responsible integration.

General-Purpose vs. Specialized Legal AI Platforms

Before evaluating individual tools, it is essential to distinguish between the two dominant categories of AI used in legal practice.

General-Purpose Large Language Models (LLMs)—such as ChatGPT and Gemini—operate as flexible, adaptive reasoning systems trained on vast volumes of publicly available data. Their defining strength lies in versatility rather than domain specificity. These models can synthesize legal concepts across jurisdictions, draft correspondence, summarize documents, translate languages, and assist with ideation across a wide range of legal tasks. Their open-ended architecture allows legal professionals to apply them creatively to novel or interdisciplinary problems that fall outside the scope of traditional legal databases.

By contrast, *Specialized Legal AI Platforms* are purpose-built applications that integrate generative AI capabilities with authoritative, curated legal datasets. These systems prioritize accuracy, citation reliability, and workflow specificity, anchoring AI outputs in verified legal sources such as statutes, case law, and regulatory materials. While less flexible than general-purpose models, they are optimized for high-stakes legal use cases where precision and accountability are paramount.

Section I: General-Purpose Large Language Models (LLMs)

ChatGPT

ChatGPT is a conversational AI developed by OpenAI and built on advanced transformer-based architectures. Although it is not trained exclusively on legal data, its strong natural language reasoning capabilities make it a versatile tool for a wide range of legal support tasks, including drafting correspondence, summarizing complex legal doctrines, and conducting preliminary research.

Features and Capabilities:

ChatGPT supports interactive dialogue, contextual continuity within sessions, and multimodal inputs, including text, code, and images. Legal professionals may create Custom GPTs tailored to firm-specific workflows, enabling automation of routine functions such as client intake, memo drafting, and internal document review. The platform also supports application programming interface (API) integrations for embedding AI functionality into existing legal systems.

Accessibility and Pricing

- **Access:** Available at www.chat.openai.com.
- **Pricing:** A free tier offers limited functionality. The Plus plan (approximately US$20 per month) provides access to flagship models, including GPT-5 and GPT-5.2. Business and Enterprise plans offer advanced administrative controls, SOC 2 compliance, and data exclusion from training—features essential for maintaining client confidentiality.

Global Reach: ChatGPT is jurisdiction-neutral and globally accessible. Its broad training data makes it particularly effective for cross-border legal concepts and multilingual translation, though outputs should always be reviewed for jurisdictional accuracy.

Gemini

Gemini is Google's generative AI platform, designed for seamless integration within the Google Workspace ecosystem. Its tight coupling with Google Docs, Gmail, and Drive makes it particularly attractive to firms already operating within Google's cloud infrastructure.

Features and Capabilities

Gemini supports document drafting, summarization, data extraction, and collaborative workflows. Legal teams may upload case files directly within their workspace to generate summaries, extract key dates, or identify salient issues, all while benefiting from Google's enterprise-grade cloud security and version control mechanisms.

Accessibility and Pricing

Access: Integrated within Google Workspace and available at www.gemini.google.com

- **Pricing:** The Google One AI Premium plan begins at approximately US$19.99 per month. Enterprise pricing is structured separately and emphasizes data governance and administrative oversight.

Global Reach: Gemini offers extensive multilingual support and global accessibility. As with all general-purpose models, outputs require jurisdictional validation in regulated legal environments.

Perplexity AI

Perplexity AI functions as a real-time answer engine that bridges traditional search and generative AI. It has gained traction in legal research for its emphasis on transparency and source attribution.

Features and Capabilities

Perplexity supports natural language queries and document uploads, returning responses accompanied by citation-linked footnotes. This allows legal professionals to verify statutes, cases, or secondary sources efficiently. Its "Pro Search" capability enables multi-step reasoning for complex legal inquiries.

Accessibility and Pricing

- **Access:** Available at www.perplexity.ai.

Pricing: A free tier is available, with a Pro plan priced at approximately US$20 per month. Enterprise offerings include API access and enhanced privacy controls.

Global Reach: Perplexity is globally accessible and jurisdiction-neutral. While its citation functionality enhances transparency, it relies primarily on publicly available sources and should not replace proprietary legal databases for authoritative precedent.

Microsoft Copilot

Microsoft Copilot is an AI assistant embedded within the Microsoft 365 suite, including Word, Excel, Outlook, and Teams. For firms operating within the Microsoft ecosystem, Copilot offers the most seamless integration into daily legal workflows.

Features and Capabilities

Copilot assists with contract drafting, document summarization, discovery review, and email management. It inherits Microsoft's enterprise-grade security architecture, ensuring that client data remains within the firm's controlled tenant environment.

Accessibility and Pricing

- **Access:** Integrated into Microsoft 365 applications and available at www.copilot.microsoft.com.

Pricing: Copilot Pro (approximately US$20 per month) is designed for individual users. Microsoft 365 Copilot for Enterprise requires a commercial subscription, typically priced around US$30 per user per month.

Global Reach: Copilot is globally deployed and designed for compliance with regulatory frameworks applicable to regulated industries, making it suitable for international legal practices.

Section II: Specialized Legal AI Tools

Lexis+ AI

Lexis+ AI is a legal-specific AI platform developed by LexisNexis that combines generative AI with authoritative legal content. Unlike general-purpose models, it operates within a closed ecosystem of vetted legal data.

Features and Capabilities

Key features include the Protégé personalized assistant, citation-verified drafting, and full-document generation for litigation and transactional work. The platform integrates with document management systems to support secure and efficient workflows.

Accessibility and Pricing

- **Access:** Available at www. lexisnexis.com.
- **Pricing:** Tiered commercial pricing varies by firm size and access level, typically ranging from approximately US$128 to US$494 per attorney per month. Full access often requires custom negotiation.

Global Reach: Lexis+ AI primarily focuses on United States and United Kingdom jurisdictions, with expanding coverage in other common law systems.

Harvey AI

Harvey AI is a bespoke AI platform designed for large law firms and corporate legal departments. It fine-tunes advanced language models using legal-specific data and a firm's internal work product.

Features and Capabilities

Harvey specializes in regulatory research, contract analysis, and high-level drafting. Its defining strength lies in its ability to internalize a firm's precedents and stylistic conventions, producing highly customized outputs.

Accessibility and Pricing

- **Access:** Available at www. harvey.ai.

Pricing: Pricing is not publicly disclosed and is negotiated on a per-firm basis, with access typically subject to waitlisting.

Global Reach: Harvey supports multi-jurisdictional deployment and is adaptable to diverse legal systems through customized training.

CoCounsel (Thomson Reuters)

CoCounsel, originally developed by Casetext and later acquired by Thomson Reuters, is positioned as an AI legal assistant optimized for reliability and task specificity.

Features and Capabilities

CoCounsel excels in discrete legal functions, including discovery review, deposition preparation, and contract policy analysis. Its integration with Westlaw and Practical Law allows it to operate within a trusted content ecosystem.

Accessibility and Pricing

- **Access:** Available at www. legal.thomsonreuters.com

Pricing: Custom pricing based on usage and firm size, with estimates ranging from approximately US$290 to US$550 per month.

Global Reach: CoCounsel is primarily focused on the United States but benefits from Thomson Reuters' expanding global infrastructure.

Clio (Manage AI and vLex Integration)

Clio has evolved from a leading cloud-based Legal Practice Management Software platform into a comprehensive intelligent legal work environment. Following its acquisition of vLex, Clio now integrates operational management with advanced legal research through Vincent AI.

Features and Capabilities

Clio's AI functionality operates across two dimensions:

- **Manage AI:** Automates administrative tasks such as scheduling, billing, deadline extraction, and client communications.
- **Vincent AI Integration:** Provides citation-verified legal research and drafting by accessing vLex's extensive global legal database.
- **Accessibility and Pricing**
- **Access:** Available at www.clio.com

Pricing: Tiered plans range from approximately US$49 to US$149 per user per month, with full Vincent AI access subject to custom negotiation.

Global Reach: Clio operates in over 130 countries and, through vLex, offers native legal research coverage across more than 110 jurisdictions, making it one of the most geographically versatile platforms available to international firms.

7

Integrating AI Into Legal Workflows

The effective integration of Artificial Intelligence (AI) into legal workflows represents a pivotal transformation in how legal professionals conduct research, manage documents, draft contracts, and engage with clients. Building on the preceding chapter, *Key AI Tools for Legal Work*, which examined leading Large Language Models such as ChatGPT, Gemini, Perplexity, and Microsoft Copilot, alongside specialized legal platforms including Lexis+ AI, Harvey AI, CoCounsel, and Clio, this chapter focuses on the practical incorporation of these technologies into everyday legal operations.

The objective is to guide law firms, corporate legal departments, and solo practitioners in adopting AI tools ethically, efficiently, and strategically. When implemented thoughtfully, AI integration enhances speed and accuracy while redefining professional competence through data-informed decision-making and improved service delivery.

Key Steps for Integrating Legal AI Tools

Successful AI adoption requires a deliberate, structured approach. The following steps outline the critical phases necessary to ensure smooth integration, regulatory compliance, and sustained productivity gains.

Step 1: Needs Assessment and Goal Definition

Before selecting any AI system, legal organizations must conduct a thorough assessment of their operational needs. For example, a litigation-focused practice may prioritize tools such as Harvey AI for discovery review, while a corporate law team may focus on Lexis+ AI for contract analysis. Solo practitioners may benefit from general-purpose models such as Gemini or Perplexity for legal research and drafting support.

Goal definition should identify specific pain points, such as repetitive drafting tasks or delayed document review, and connect them to measurable objectives, for example reducing turnaround time by a defined percentage or improving research accuracy and consistency.

Step 2: Selection of Appropriate Tools

Selecting the appropriate AI tools depends on factors such as budget, jurisdictional coverage, data sensitivity, and task specialization. Lexis+ AI excels in authoritative legal research, CoCounsel supports automated document analysis, and Clio enables practice management integration. For cost-efficient versatility, general-purpose LLMs such as ChatGPT or Gemini can support a wide range of legal functions.

This selection process should include pilot testing, stakeholder feedback, and technical compatibility reviews to ensure alignment with existing systems and workflows.

Step 3: Data Preparation and Security Compliance

Integrating AI systems necessitates rigorous data governance. Law firms must ensure that confidential case materials, contracts, and client communications are handled in compliance with applicable data protection laws and professional conduct obligations. Secure data storage, encryption, access controls, and anonymization where appropriate should be standard practice.

Platforms such as Microsoft Copilot, when deployed within Microsoft 365 enterprise environments, offer security architectures aligned with organizational compliance standards, allowing legal professionals to leverage AI capabilities while maintaining confidentiality and regulatory compliance.

Step 4: Workflow Integration and Customization

Once selected, AI tools should be seamlessly embedded into existing workflows. For example, CoCounsel may be integrated into case management systems for document review, while ChatGPT, Gemini, or Perplexity can be accessed via application programming interfaces to support research and drafting processes. Developing standardized prompt templates tailored to specific practice areas or case types further promotes consistency, efficiency, and quality control across teams.

Step 5: Ongoing Monitoring and Evaluation

AI deployment requires continuous oversight. Firms should track performance indicators such as output accuracy, turnaround time, and user satisfaction. Regular reviews, system updates, and retraining sessions are essential to maintaining effectiveness. Where performance issues arise, such as declining retrieval accuracy, prompt refinement or data source updates may be necessary.

Best Practices for Successful Integration

Integrating AI into legal practice involves more than technological adoption; it requires organizational, cultural, and ethical alignment. The following best practices support sustainable and responsible use.

1. Establish Clear Governance and Ethical Policies

Firms should define clear internal policies governing how AI outputs are generated, validated, stored, and relied upon. These policies must align with professional conduct rules, bar association guidance, and applicable regulatory requirements to preserve client trust and ethical accountability.

2. Prioritize Data Privacy and Confidentiality

Data privacy and client confidentiality are paramount. Legal professionals must ensure that no client-identifiable or privileged information is disclosed to unsecured or non-compliant third-party platforms. AI solutions offering enterprise-level security, including Perplexity Enterprise Max, Microsoft Copilot, and ChatGPT Business or Enterprise, provide privacy-controlled environments suitable for handling sensitive legal data.

3. Conduct Staff Training and Continuous Support

Ongoing training is essential to maximizing the value of AI tools. Firms should provide structured instruction on tool usage, ethical considerations, and compliance obligations. Equally important is developing proficiency in communicating effectively with AI systems. Part III of this book, which addresses Legal Prompt Engineering, provides detailed guidance on prompt design, structure, and common errors.

4. Start with Pilot Programs

Before full-scale deployment, AI tools should be tested in controlled environments or within specific departments. Pilot programs help identify technical limitations, workflow mismatches, or ethical concerns early, enabling informed adjustments before broader adoption.

5. Maintain Human Oversight

Despite advances in automation, human judgment remains central to legal practice. Lawyers must review and validate all AI-generated outputs, including drafts, summaries, and analyses, before relying on them for legal advice or client communication. Continuous human oversight ensures alignment with legal standards and professional discretion.

Legal Use Cases for AI Tools

AI technologies are reshaping modern legal practice by improving precision, efficiency, and strategic insight across multiple workflows. The following examples illustrate how AI enhances specific areas of legal practice.

Document Review and Contract Analysis

AI has significantly transformed document and contract review, traditionally among the most time-intensive legal tasks. Tools such as Harvey AI and CoCounsel automate clause extraction, risk identification, and deviation analysis across large document sets, enhancing consistency and compliance.

For solo and small firms, ChatGPT and Perplexity provide cost-effective assistance with drafting agreements, summarizing legal terms, and preparing standard clauses. Gemini adds value through contextual reasoning, while Microsoft Copilot enables seamless drafting and editing within Word and Excel, supporting lawyers who operate extensively within Microsoft 365 environments.

Legal Research and Case Prediction

AI-powered legal research tools dramatically reduce the time required to locate relevant authorities. Lexis+ AI leverages natural language processing to retrieve contextually relevant case law and commentary from proprietary databases.
General-purpose LLMs such as ChatGPT and Perplexity support research planning, case summarization, and memorandum drafting. Gemini excels at synthesizing complex legal issues and identifying patterns across precedent, supporting analytical and strategic legal work.

AI-Powered Litigation Support

In litigation, AI assists with discovery, document management, and case preparation. Harvey AI and CoCounsel streamline discovery review, identify key evidence, and support brief drafting. For smaller teams, ChatGPT aids in preparing motions and procedural documents, while Perplexity and Gemini accelerate trial research and strategy development, allowing lawyers to focus on advocacy and courtroom preparation.

Compliance and Regulatory Monitoring

In regulatory practice, AI tools support monitoring legislative changes and compliance obligations. Lexis+ AI and Clio track regulatory updates and assist with compliance audits. ChatGPT and Gemini help summarize new regulations and map obligations to operational processes. Microsoft Copilot integrates these outputs into structured reports, presentations, and dashboards, streamlining compliance documentation.

Client Communication and Advisory Automation

AI also enhances client communication. ChatGPT and Gemini assist in drafting client updates, summaries, and advisories in clear, accessible language. Microsoft Copilot, integrated with Outlook and Teams, supports communication management and follow-up, while Clio organizes client records and automates intake workflows. Together, these tools improve client engagement while reducing administrative burden.

Copyrighted Material

Conclusion

Integrating AI into legal workflows is no longer optional; it is a defining feature of modern legal practice. When implemented strategically, AI enhances productivity, reduces operational costs, and improves accuracy across advisory, transactional, and litigation contexts. By combining strong governance, ethical oversight, and continuous training, legal professionals can achieve a balanced synergy between human expertise and computational intelligence.

Ultimately, AI integration represents not merely an operational improvement but a paradigm shift toward a more intelligent and data-driven legal ecosystem. Firms that embrace this transformation will be best positioned to thrive in a future where legal excellence depends not only on precedent and advocacy, but also on the responsible and effective use of intelligent systems. The next chapter, *Evaluating and Selecting Legal AI Tools,* builds on this foundation by guiding practitioners through the critical process of assessing and choosing AI solutions tailored to their specific professional needs.

8

Evaluating and Selecting Legal AI Tools

The integration of Artificial Intelligence (AI) into the legal profession has fundamentally reshaped how legal services are delivered, enabling greater efficiency, precision, and strategic insight. Building on the previous chapter, *Integrating AI into Legal Workflows,* which examined practical approaches to embedding AI into daily legal operations, this chapter advances the discussion by providing a structured framework for evaluating and selecting appropriate legal AI tools.

Selecting the right AI solution is a critical strategic decision influenced by factors such as firm size, practice area specialization, jurisdictional focus, data sensitivity, and budgetary constraints. Large and multinational firms often benefit from enterprise-grade platforms such as Harvey AI, CoCounsel, or Lexis+ AI, which are purpose-built for advanced legal research, contract analysis, and litigation support. By contrast, small firms and solo practitioners frequently adopt more adaptable and cost-efficient solutions such as ChatGPT, Perplexity, Gemini, and Microsoft Copilot, which deliver substantial value in drafting, summarization, and general legal analysis.

This chapter presents a comparative overview of specialized legal AI platforms and general-purpose productivity tools, followed by a set of evaluative criteria designed to assist practitioners in selecting solutions that align with their operational, regulatory, and professional requirements.

Table 1.1: Functional Comparison – Specialized Legal AI Platforms

Use Case	Lexis+ AI	Harvey AI	CoCounsel (Thomson Reuters)	Clio (+ vLex/Vincent AI)
Legal Research	Retrieval-augmented research integrated with proprietary LexisNexis databases, including citation validation.	Contextual research and document synthesis, with growing strength in regulatory analysis.	Deep Research. AI-assisted internal research integrated with Westlaw Precision for case mapping	Vincent AI integration enables natural language research across more than one billion documents from over 110 jurisdictions
Contract Review	Automated clause extraction and benchmarking against precedent and market standards.	Designed for due diligence, compliance checks, and large-scale drafting recommendations..	Summarization and deviation detection against firm-specific playbooks.	Supports full contract lifecycle management, including templates and electronic signatures.

Use Case	Lexis+ AI	Harvey AI	CoCounsel (Thomson Reuters)	Clio (+ vLex/Vincent AI)
Litigation Support	Predictive insights on judicial behavior and case outcomes, with litigation brief generation.	Produces complex motions, pleadings, and witness statements with contextual reasoning.	Assists with deposition preparation, timelines, and evidence linkage.	Centralized case tracking, billing, client communication, and docket automation.
Jurisdictional Reach	Strong coverage in the United States, United Kingdom, Canada, and Australia.	Expanding coverage across the United States, United Kingdom, European Union, India, and Singapore.	Core strength in the United States, United Kingdom, and Canada, with expansion into European and Asian markets.	Global adoption with General Data Protection Regulation compliance and extensive international law coverage through vLex.

Table 1.2: Functional Comparison – General-Purpose & Productivity AI Tools

Use Case	ChatGPT (OpenAI)	Perplexity AI	Gemini (Google)	Microsoft Copilot
Legal Research	Explains concepts, generates research outlines, and summarizes transcripts, with hallucination risk if unchecked.	Provides concise answers supported by citations from live web data, well-suited for initial fact-finding.	Analyzes large volumes of documents using extensive context windows, including uploaded files.	Summarizes internal firm data alongside web results within Microsoft 365 environments.
Contract Review	Assists with initial clause drafting and language simplification.	Locates comparative clauses and definitions from public sources.	Identifies obligations and risks within uploaded contracts via Google Drive integration.	Automates review, formatting, and clause management directly within Word.
Litigation Support	Drafts discovery requests, summarizes depositions, and suggests cross-examination questions.	Rapid verification of public records, dates, and events.	Identifies argument patterns across extensive case histories provided by the user.	Summarizes Teams meetings, organizes Outlook threads, and drafts case updates.
Jurisdictional Reach	Globally accessible but lacks native jurisdiction-specific databases.	Domain filtering enables jurisdiction-specific web searches.	Strong multilingual capabilities with broad global reach.	Available worldwide with configurable data residency options for regulatory compliance.

Key Considerations for Selecting an AI Tool

Selecting an AI solution requires deliberate analysis of factors that affect usability, compliance, and long-term strategic value. The following considerations provide a structured framework for informed decision-making.

1. Functionality

Functionality defines the core value of any AI tool. Legal professionals must assess whether a platform adequately supports their primary practice areas, whether litigation, transactional work, compliance, or advisory services. Specialized tools such as Harvey AI and CoCounsel excel in complex legal reasoning, regulatory analysis, and high-volume document review. General-purpose tools such as ChatGPT and Gemini are better suited for drafting correspondence, summarizing legal concepts, and supporting preliminary research.

Aligning tool capabilities with workflow requirements minimizes inefficiencies and prevents over-investment in underutilized features.

2. Cost and Return on Investment (ROI)

Cost considerations extend beyond subscription fees to include licensing models, scalability, and long-term value. Smaller practices may favor cost-efficient tools such as Perplexity or ChatGPT Plus, which deliver high utility without enterprise-level expense. Larger firms can often justify the higher investment in Lexis+ AI or Harvey AI due to their advanced analytics, proprietary datasets, and secure integrations.

Return on investment should be evaluated holistically, accounting for improvements in accuracy, turnaround time, risk reduction, and client satisfaction.

3. Ease of Integration

Seamless integration with existing systems is essential for successful adoption. Platforms such as Clio, enhanced by vLex integration, bridge practice management and legal research within a unified ecosystem. CoCounsel offers robust application programming interfaces for document management integration, while Microsoft Copilot embeds AI functionality directly into widely used tools such as Word, Outlook, and Excel.

Tools that integrate naturally into established workflows reduce training overhead and accelerate adoption.

4. Jurisdictional and Data Compliance

Jurisdictional relevance and regulatory compliance are non-negotiable considerations. Tools such as Lexis+ AI and vLex provide jurisdiction-specific legal content grounded in authoritative sources, ensuring research outputs are relevant and reliable. Practice management platforms such as Clio support global use while maintaining compliance with data protection frameworks including the General Data Protection Regulation and the California Consumer Privacy Act.

Firms must ensure that any AI tool supports applicable jurisdictions and adheres to data protection and professional confidentiality obligations.

5. Scalability

Scalability ensures that AI solutions can evolve alongside firm growth. Platforms such as Clio and Harvey AI offer modular expansions, enabling access to additional features such as automated discovery or advanced analytics as needs change. Scalable solutions should support multi-user environments, interoperability with emerging technologies, and regular updates aligned with legal and regulatory developments.

6. Staff Training and Support

The effectiveness of AI adoption depends heavily on user competence. Firms should prioritize tools that offer structured onboarding, ongoing training resources, and responsive vendor support. Platforms such as Microsoft Copilot and Clio provide integrated learning materials, while Lexis+ AI offers dedicated customer success programs for enterprise users.

Adequate training and support reduce the risk of misuse, enhance productivity, and reinforce ethical and compliant use.

Conclusion

Evaluating and selecting legal AI tools is a pivotal step in the transformation of modern legal practice. By systematically assessing functionality, cost, integration, jurisdictional compliance, scalability, and training support, legal professionals can make informed decisions that enhance efficiency, accuracy, and client service.

Specialized platforms such as Lexis+ AI, Harvey AI, and CoCounsel deliver targeted capabilities for research, contract analysis, and litigation support, while general-purpose tools such as ChatGPT, Gemini, Perplexity, and Microsoft Copilot provide flexible and cost-effective solutions for routine legal tasks.

Ultimately, effective AI adoption balances technological sophistication with contextual awareness, ensuring that selected tools align with firm objectives, jurisdictional obligations, and professional ethics. When chosen thoughtfully, legal AI systems become not merely operational aids but strategic partners in the evolving delivery of legal services.

9

Limitations of AI In Legal Practice

As discussed in the preceding chapters, the integration of advanced systems such as Lexis+ AI, Harvey AI, CoCounsel, and Clio has significantly transformed legal research, document management, and client service delivery. These technologies enhance efficiency, reduce administrative burden, and expand analytical capacity. Nevertheless, artificial intelligence remains a tool, powerful but inherently limited. Its outputs are constrained by training data, contextual scope, model architecture, and probabilistic reasoning.

This chapter examines the structural, ethical, and practical limitations of artificial intelligence in legal practice. By clearly identifying where caution, verification, and professional judgment must prevail, legal practitioners can deploy AI responsibly while maintaining ethical integrity, accuracy, and jurisdictional compliance.

1. Data Privacy and Confidentiality Risks

Most legal AI tools operate within cloud-based infrastructures, raising persistent concerns regarding client confidentiality, legal privilege, and regulatory compliance. Lawyers are subject to stringent professional obligations to safeguard client information, and the submission of confidential materials to public or consumer-grade AI systems may constitute a waiver of privilege.

To mitigate these risks, firms should restrict usage to enterprise-grade or business-tier platforms that contractually guarantee zero data retention and prohibit model training on user inputs. Even within such environments, highly sensitive personally identifiable information should be redacted where feasible. Additionally, firms should conduct periodic vendor due diligence and audits to confirm ongoing compliance with applicable data protection frameworks, including the General Data Protection Regulation, the California Consumer Privacy Act, and sector-specific confidentiality requirements.

2. Bias and Fairness in AI-Assisted Decision-Making

Artificial intelligence systems inevitably reflect the biases embedded within their training data. Historical distortions in sentencing patterns, enforcement practices, or demographic representation may be reproduced or amplified by AI-driven tools, particularly those offering predictive analytics or outcome forecasting.

This risk is especially acute when AI is used to assess litigation strategy or settlement exposure. To address this, firms must adopt a strict human-in-the-loop approach, ensuring that AI-generated assessments are reviewed critically and never treated as determinative. Preference should be given to vendors that publicly disclose their responsible AI frameworks, bias mitigation strategies, and model governance practices. Any AI-generated risk assessment should be treated as an indicative analytical aid rather than an authoritative judgment.

3. Limited Contextual and Normative Understanding

Despite their linguistic sophistication, AI systems lack true contextual comprehension and normative reasoning. They do not understand legislative intent, judicial discretion, or the broader policy objectives underlying legal rules. As a result, AI may misinterpret nuanced contractual provisions, overlook emerging judicial trends, or fail to account for unreported decisions that materially alter the legal landscape.

Accordingly, AI should be deployed as a drafting and summarization assistant, not as an interpretive authority. Legal professionals must supply precise contextual constraints through deliberate prompting, anchoring outputs to specific jurisdictions, statutes, and doctrinal frameworks. Narrow, well-defined instructions significantly reduce the risk of generic or misleading outputs and enhance analytical relevance.

4. Regulatory and Ethical Constraints

The absence of harmonized global standards for legal AI complicates regulatory compliance. High-profile judicial sanctions for unverified AI-generated citations illustrate the professional consequences of careless reliance on automated outputs. Courts and professional bodies increasingly expect lawyers to verify all submissions and, in some jurisdictions, to disclose the use of AI in legal drafting.

A "trust but verify" approach is therefore essential. Every citation, quotation, and factual assertion produced by AI must be independently validated against primary sources, such as official court databases or statutory repositories. Where disclosure obligations exist, practitioners must be prepared to acknowledge AI assistance transparently and accurately.

5. Jurisdictional and Territorial Limitations

Although many AI tools are expanding their geographic coverage, jurisdictional precision remains uneven. General-purpose models may inadvertently apply legal principles from one jurisdiction to another if not explicitly constrained, resulting in inaccurate or misleading analysis.

To prevent jurisdictional drift, practitioners should confirm the scope, training data, and jurisdictional filters available within a given platform before use. For cross-border matters, specialized systems that allow strict regional filtering are preferable, as they reduce the risk of conflating legal doctrines across jurisdictions and enhance doctrinal reliability.

6. Dependence on Data Quality

AI outputs are only as reliable as the data upon which they rely. If an underlying database contains outdated statutes, repealed regulations, or superseded case law, the resulting analysis may be confidently presented yet substantively incorrect. This risk is particularly pronounced in rapidly evolving areas of law.

Legal professionals must therefore verify the currency of AI-generated material and treat AI primarily as a preliminary drafting aid. Final validation should always involve traditional citators or authoritative legal research tools to confirm that all referenced authorities remain valid and applicable.

7. Hallucinations in Legal Outputs

In legal contexts, hallucinations manifest in two principal forms. Citation hallucinations involve the fabrication of non-existent cases or authorities, while reasoning hallucinations occur when real cases are cited but inaccurately interpreted. Both pose serious professional risks.

Mitigation requires a structured review process in which every AI output is scrutinized for both factual existence and doctrinal accuracy. Tools that provide direct links to source materials facilitate efficient verification and should be prioritized for professional use.

8. Integration Challenges and Professional Skill Atrophy

Excessive reliance on AI may contribute to skill atrophy, particularly among junior lawyers who risk bypassing foundational research and analytical training. Poorly planned implementation may also result in fragmented workflows and data silos.

To address these concerns, firms should adopt phased deployment strategies, initially limiting AI usage to low-risk tasks before expanding to substantive legal work. Importantly, AI should be positioned as a pedagogical aid that critiques and refines human work, rather than a substitute for legal reasoning. This approach preserves professional development while enhancing efficiency.

Conclusion

Artificial intelligence has irrevocably reshaped contemporary legal practice, offering unprecedented gains in efficiency, accessibility, and analytical support. Yet, as this chapter demonstrates, its deployment is accompanied by inherent limitations, ranging from data privacy risks and algorithmic bias to jurisdictional ambiguity and hallucinated outputs. These constraints reaffirm a foundational principle: AI augments legal reasoning, but it does not replace professional judgment.

Critically, the effectiveness of AI in legal practice depends not solely on the sophistication of the tool, but on the competence of the user. The ability to constrain outputs, define legal context, and critically interrogate results is now an essential professional skill.

For this reason, responsible AI adoption is inseparable from mastery of prompting techniques. The next section of this book, *Part III: Legal Prompt Engineering,* moves from diagnosis to solution. It provides practical frameworks, structured methodologies, and advanced prompts designed to transform generalist AI systems into precise, reliable, and ethically compliant legal assistants.

Part III

Mastering Legal Prompt Engineering

What is Prompt Engineering in Legal Work?

Prompt engineering is the strategic discipline of designing precise and purposeful instructions that guide artificial intelligence systems toward accurate, relevant, and contextually appropriate outputs. Within the legal domain, it functions as the critical translation layer between human legal reasoning and machine-generated responses.

For legal professionals, mastery of prompt engineering is transformative. It shifts artificial intelligence from a passive information retrieval tool into an active analytical collaborator capable of producing structured drafts, nuanced legal reasoning, and strategic guidance. For example, when drafting a contractual provision, a lawyer may instruct a large language model to consider not only the subject matter, but also the governing law, jurisdiction, drafting tone, commercial context, and allocation of risk between the parties.

While specialized platforms such as Harvey AI or CoCounsel embed predefined prompt frameworks to streamline recurring workflows, the ability to craft bespoke prompts remains indispensable for complex, non-standard, or jurisdiction-specific legal work. This chapter categorizes legal prompts by purpose and cognitive complexity, offering a practical framework for their effective application.

Categories of Legal Prompts by Purpose and Complexity

Legal prompts can be broadly categorized as follows:

- **Task-Oriented Prompts:** Direct, narrowly scoped instructions focused on discrete legal tasks such as drafting, reviewing, or summarizing.
- **Creative Prompts:** Designed to generate alternative arguments, persuasive narratives, or innovative contractual language.
- **Problem-Solving Prompts:** Structured to analyze complex factual scenarios and recommend legal outcomes or strategies.
- **Conversational Prompts:** Used to simulate client consultations, internal discussions, or adversarial exchanges.
- **Analytical Prompts:** Intended to extract patterns, synthesize authorities, or evaluate trends across legal data.

Each category supports different phases of legal work, ranging from research and drafting to strategic planning and client engagement. The sections that follow examine their practical application.

Task-Oriented Prompts for Specific Legal Tasks

Task-oriented prompts form the foundation of AI-assisted legal workflows. They instruct the model to perform clearly defined legal actions while adhering to explicit constraints. Precision in these prompts is essential to ensure jurisdictional accuracy, professional tone, and doctrinal relevance.

> ***Example Prompt***
> *"Draft a confidentiality clause for a joint venture agreement under English law. The clause must specify non-disclosure obligations, a duration of five years, and explicit exceptions for disclosures required by law."*

By clearly defining the task (drafting), jurisdiction (English law), and constraints (duration and exceptions), the prompt minimizes ambiguity and produces a clause suitable for professional refinement. This approach significantly reduces the risk of generic or jurisdictionally inappropriate drafting.

Creative Prompts for Strategic Innovation

Creative prompts encourage artificial intelligence to explore alternative perspectives, simulate professional personas, and generate persuasive or unconventional legal strategies. These prompts are particularly valuable in negotiation planning, advocacy, and complex dispute resolution.

Example Prompt

"Assume the role of senior buyer's counsel in a merger and acquisition transaction. Draft three distinct opening negotiation positions regarding the purchase price:

1. *A firm, non-negotiable offer grounded in current market valuations.*
2. *A collaborative strategy emphasizing long-term partnership potential.*
3. *A data-driven argument referencing recent market volatility to justify a 20 percent valuation adjustment."*

This prompt instructs the AI to adopt a defined professional persona and apply multiple negotiation strategies. The resulting output provides the lawyer with a range of tactical options, facilitating strategic decision-making beyond routine legal analysis.

Problem-Solving Prompts in Legal Scenarios

Problem-solving prompts assist lawyers in structuring legal analysis around complex fact patterns, closely mirroring traditional analytical frameworks such as Issue, Rule, Analysis, and Conclusion (IRAC). These prompts require the AI to balance legal doctrine with factual reasoning.

Example Prompt
"You are an experienced legal analyst. Based on the following facts, identify potential causes of action, applicable defenses, and available remedies under general contract law principles.

Facts: A supplier failed to deliver specialized equipment, citing unforeseen manufacturing delays. The buyer incurred operational losses and seeks legal recourse.

Present your analysis under the following headings:

1. *Causes of Action*
2. *Defenses (with specific reference to force majeure)*
3. *Remedies"*

By explicitly structuring the output, the prompt compels the model to compartmentalize its reasoning and consider both claims and counterclaims. This results in a balanced, memo-ready analysis suitable for professional review.

Conversational Prompts in Legal Consultations

Conversational prompts simulate interactive dialogues and are particularly effective for preparing client consultations, internal briefings, or adversarial questioning. They allow lawyers to rehearse explanations, anticipate concerns, and refine communication strategies.

Example Prompt

"Act as a senior legal consultant conducting an initial consultation with a small business owner facing a potential breach of an employment contract. Ask clarifying questions sequentially, explain relevant legal concepts in plain language, and conclude with a summary of recommended next steps."

By instructing the AI to engage interactively rather than respond in a single output, the prompt transforms the model into a simulated professional counterpart. This approach helps lawyers identify informational gaps and improve the structure of real-world consultations.

Analytical Prompts for Legal Research and Insights

Analytical prompts direct artificial intelligence to synthesize, compare, and interpret legal materials. They are best suited for transforming large volumes of legal information into structured insights.

Example Prompt

"Analyze the development of data protection enforcement in the European Union from 2018 to 2024, with particular emphasis on the impact of the General Data Protection Regulation on penalties for cross-border data transfers. Present your findings under the following headings:

1. *Legislative Baseline*
2. *Key Judicial Interpretations*
3. *Implications for Corporate Compliance"*

Segmenting analytical tasks into defined sections prevents unfocused responses and produces outputs that can be readily incorporated into research memoranda, advisory notes, or policy briefings.

Conclusion

Legal prompt engineering transforms artificial intelligence from a passive information source into an active reasoning partner. Each category of prompt—task-oriented, creative, problem-solving, conversational, and analytical—serves a distinct cognitive function within legal practice. Mastery of these techniques enables lawyers to obtain outputs that are precise, contextually grounded, and ethically sound.

As artificial intelligence continues to evolve, the ability to design effective prompts will become a core professional competency rather than a technical novelty. Lawyers who refine this skill will be better positioned to integrate AI responsibly, enhance analytical rigor, and maintain professional judgment in an increasingly technology-driven legal landscape.

11

Key Elements of Effective Legal Prompts

Effective legal prompting is both a technical skill and a disciplined professional practice. It requires the formulation of precise, structured instructions that enable Large Language Models—such as ChatGPT, Gemini, Perplexity AI, and Microsoft Copilot—to generate accurate, relevant, and dependable legal outputs. These elements are essential to ensuring that AI-generated responses align with legal reasoning, professional ethics, and factual reliability.

Prompt engineering in legal practice differs fundamentally from general-purpose prompting. Legal prompts must reflect doctrinal logic, jurisdictional boundaries, document typology, and procedural context. A prompt designed for case law analysis, for example, differs materially from one intended to draft a non-disclosure agreement or conduct a regulatory compliance review.

This chapter examines seven core elements of effective legal prompts: specificity, clarity, context, relevance, conciseness, constraints, and consistency. Each element is explained with a practical example to support systematic, high-quality interaction with Large Language Models in legal work.

1. Specificity

Specificity ensures that the AI focuses precisely on the intended legal objective. Prompts that lack specificity often result in vague, overly generalized responses—a phenomenon sometimes described as *"hallucinated competence."* For legal professionals, specificity requires clearly defining the legal domain, task, jurisdiction, and expected output format.

> ***Example Prompt***
> *"You are a contract law expert. Draft a confidentiality clause for a technology licensing agreement governed by English law. Ensure the clause includes defined scope limitations, a five-year duration, and explicit exceptions for court-ordered disclosures."*

This prompt establishes a clear role (contract law expert), task (drafting), and framework (English law with defined constraints). Large Language Models perform most reliably when variables are tightly scoped, reducing ambiguity and minimizing the risk of generic or jurisdictionally inappropriate drafting.

2. Clarity

Clarity emphasizes linguistic precision and logical structure. Ambiguous phrasing undermines accuracy and can cause the model to misinterpret the task or dilute the relevance of its response. Effective legal prompts use direct instructions, active verbs, and concise sentence construction.

Example Prompt

"Summarize the legal reasoning in the Supreme Court of Canada's decision in R. v. Jordan (2016). Focus specifically on how the decision redefined the right to a trial within a reasonable time under the Canadian Charter of Rights and Freedoms."

This prompt directs the model toward a specific analytical lens rather than a general case summary. By avoiding vague language such as "tell me about," the lawyer ensures that the AI concentrates on doctrinal impact rather than peripheral facts.

3. Context

Context defines the factual, procedural, or commercial environment within which the AI must operate. Without sufficient context, even advanced models tend to produce abstract or generic advice that fails to address the client's actual circumstances.

Example Prompt

"You are assisting a corporate lawyer preparing for a merger between two United States–based software companies. Identify the key antitrust compliance considerations under the Sherman Act and the Federal Trade Commission Act, and outline sector-specific due diligence steps."

By supplying contextual markers—jurisdiction, transaction type, and industry sector—the prompt anchors the model's reasoning. This ensures that the output addresses technology-sector concerns, such as intellectual property concentration, rather than generic merger issues.

4. Relevance (Negative Prompting)

Relevance ensures that the AI's output remains tightly aligned with the task at hand. One effective technique is *negative prompting*: explicitly instructing the model on what to exclude.

> ***Example Prompt***
>
> *"Provide a list of applicable obligations under the European Union's General Data Protection Regulation for a law firm offering cross-border cloud storage services. Exclude unrelated cybersecurity frameworks such as ISO 27001, and focus solely on General Data Protection Regulation provisions governing international data transfers."*

The exclusionary instruction enforces topical discipline. In regulatory research—where multiple legal regimes frequently intersect—negative prompting prevents conflation and significantly improves analytical precision.

5. Conciseness

Conciseness ensures that prompts are comprehensive without being excessive. Legal professionals should aim for a balance that provides sufficient direction while avoiding unnecessary detail that distracts from the core task.

Example Prompt

"Draft a concise explanation distinguishing tort liability from contractual liability under Australian law. Limit the response to 150 words."

The imposed word limit compels the model to prioritize doctrinal essentials. Conciseness is particularly valuable when generating executive summaries, client communications, or advisory memoranda.

6. Constraints

Constraints define non-negotiable parameters governing tone, structure, citation style, length, or formatting. They are critical for ensuring that AI-generated outputs conform to professional legal standards.

Example Prompt

"Prepare a summary of Donoghue v. Stevenson (1932) in a formal academic tone. Use OSCOLA citation style for all references. Limit the response to two paragraphs."

By specifying tone and citation format, the prompt produces an output suitable for academic or professional publication. Consistent use of constraints enables predictable, repeatable results—an essential requirement in legal drafting and publishing.

7. Consistency

Consistency ensures stylistic and logical uniformity across multiple AI-generated documents. This is particularly important in large-scale projects such as contract suites, policy manuals, or recurring client communications.

> ***Example Prompt***
>
> *"Using the same structure, tone, and clause numbering as the employment contract previously drafted, generate a non-disclosure agreement for the same employee."*

This instruction leverages the model's contextual memory to replicate established drafting conventions. Consistency reduces post-editing time and enhances professional coherence across document sets.

Conclusion

Effective legal prompt engineering rests on seven foundational pillars: specificity, clarity, context, relevance, conciseness, constraints, and consistency. When applied systematically, these principles transform Large Language Models from conversational tools into reliable, ethical, and professionally aligned legal collaborators.

Mastery of these elements does not eliminate the need for legal judgment; rather, it amplifies it. By controlling inputs with precision and discipline, legal professionals can harness artificial intelligence as a force multiplier—enhancing accuracy, efficiency, and analytical depth while preserving the core values of the legal profession.

12

Advanced Legal Prompting Techniques

Building on the foundational principles of specificity, clarity, and context, advanced legal prompting enables practitioners to deliberately guide a Large Language Model's (LLM's) reasoning process, replicate expert-level analytical judgment, and significantly improve the reliability of AI-generated legal outputs.

Where basic prompting merely instructs an AI to *perform a task,* advanced prompting designs the cognitive pathway the model follows to reach its conclusion. These techniques—Zero-Shot Prompting, Few-Shot Prompting, Chain-of-Thought Prompting, Iterative Prompting, and Prompt Chaining—allow lawyers to tailor AI interaction to the complexity of the legal issue at hand. Used effectively, they reposition AI from a drafting assistant to a structured legal analyst.

Zero-Shot Prompting

Zero-shot prompting involves issuing a task without providing examples or stylistic guidance. The AI relies entirely on its pre-trained knowledge to generate a response. This method is best suited to scenarios requiring quick explanations of settled legal principles or foundational definitions.

> ***Example Prompt***
> *"Define the doctrine of consideration under English contract law and explain its three essential elements."*

Zero-shot prompting is efficient for *black-letter law* questions where doctrinal contours are stable and widely accepted. However, it carries higher risk in nuanced drafting, jurisdiction-sensitive analysis, or stylistic work, where the absence of guidance can lead to generic or imprecise output.

Few-Shot Prompting

Few-shot prompting improves precision by supplying the model with a limited number of representative examples that illustrate the desired structure, tone, or substantive approach. In legal practice, this closely mirrors the use of precedents.

> ***Example Prompt***
> *"I will provide two examples of confidentiality clauses. Using these as stylistic and structural references, draft a similar clause for a consulting agreement involving trade secrets.*
> *Example 1: 'The receiving party shall not disclose proprietary information...'*
> *Example 2: 'All confidential data must be safeguarded through secure storage...'*
> ***Task:*** *Draft the new clause ."*

Few-shot prompting is particularly effective for enforcing firm-specific drafting conventions, formatting standards, and stylistic consistency. By demonstrating what an acceptable outcome looks like, lawyers significantly reduce the need for post-generation editing.

Chain-of-Thought Prompting

Chain-of-Thought (CoT) prompting compels the model to articulate its reasoning through a structured sequence of logical steps rather than delivering a conclusory answer. This approach closely parallels the IRAC method (Issue, Rule, Analysis, Conclusion) taught in legal education.

> ***Example Prompt***
> *"Analyze whether an electronically signed contract satisfies enforceability requirements under the UK law. Do not provide a conclusory answer. Instead, explain your reasoning step by step:*
>
> 1. *Identify the relevant statute.*
> 2. *Analyze the requirements relating to intent and consent.*
> 3. *Assess the validity of the specific signature method.*
> 4. *Conclude on enforceability."*

Chain-of-Thought prompting is indispensable for complex legal analysis. By requiring the model to "show its work," it exposes reasoning errors, misapplied statutes, or faulty assumptions that might otherwise remain hidden in a summary response.

Iterative Prompting

Iterative prompting relies on multi-turn interaction, allowing the user to refine outputs progressively. This mirrors the traditional supervisory relationship in legal practice: draft, review, feedback, and revision.

> ***Example Prompt Sequence***
>
> *Turn 1: "Summarize the main obligations of data controllers under the GDPR."*
>
> *Turn 2: "Good. Now expand the summary to include specific enforcement mechanisms under Articles 77–84."*
>
> *Turn 3: "Finalize this by converting the summary into a concise compliance checklist suitable for internal policy documentation."*

Iterative prompting acknowledges that high-quality legal work rarely emerges in a single draft. Treating the AI as a collaborative assistant—rather than expecting a perfect one-shot response—allows for layered refinement and greater doctrinal precision.

Prompt Chaining

Prompt chaining links multiple prompts so that the output of one becomes the structured input for the next. This technique is ideal for managing complex, multi-stage legal workflows.

> ***Example Prompt Chain***
>
> *Step 1: "Summarize the key risk clauses in this commercial lease agreement."*
>
> *Step 2: "Using that summary, identify which specific clauses pose a financial risk to the tenant."*
>
> *Step 3: "For each identified risk, propose mitigation strategies and draft suggested redlines."*

Prompt chaining is particularly effective in due diligence, regulatory assessments, and transactional review. Breaking complex tasks into discrete stages prevents cognitive overload and enables deeper analysis at each step.

Table 2.1: Advanced Legal Prompting Matrix

Prompting Technique	Purpose	Legal Use Case	Key Advantages
Zero-Shot Prompting	Generate response using training data only.	Definitions, foundational explanations	Speed and efficiency for settled law
Few-Shot Prompting	Guide style and structure using examples	Clause drafting, citation formatting	Ensures stylistic and structural consistency
Chain-of-Thought Prompting	Enforce step-by-step reasoning	Statutory interpretation, case analysis	Makes logic transparent; reduces hallucinations
Iterative Prompting	Refine output through feedback loops	Memo polishing, tone adjustment	Enables precision and controlled revision
Prompt Chaining	Sequence multi-stage tasks	Due diligence, risk assessment	Manages complexity through structured decomposition.

Conclusion

Advanced legal prompting techniques allow practitioners to move beyond superficial interaction toward deliberate reasoning control. The ability to select and combine methods—such as using Few-Shot prompting for drafting and Chain-of-Thought prompting for legal analysis—enables lawyers to shape both the depth and reliability of AI outputs.

When applied strategically, these techniques transform Large Language Models from passive information tools into dynamic analytical collaborators. Mastery of advanced prompting is therefore not a technical luxury, but an emerging core competency for legal professionals operating in an AI-augmented practice environment.

13

Assigning Roles In Legal Prompts

Role-based prompting—often referred to as ***persona engineering***—is a high-impact technique for achieving contextual precision in AI-assisted legal work. It involves explicitly defining the professional identity, level of seniority, or analytical stance the AI should adopt before performing a task.

In legal practice, generic prompts tend to produce generic, "law student–level" responses. By assigning a role, the practitioner directs the model to emulate the reasoning patterns, vocabulary, ethical sensitivities, and risk posture of a specific legal actor—such as a senior mergers and acquisitions partner, a skeptical appellate judge, or a data protection officer operating under the General Data Protection Regulation. This framing primes the model to generate outputs that align more closely with real-world professional expectations.

This section examines three foundational role-based prompting techniques used in legal AI practice: the Role (Identity) technique, the Act As (Behavioral) technique, and the Assume (Perspective) technique.

The "Role" Technique (Identity-Based Prompting)

The "Role" technique instructs the AI to adopt a defined professional identity before generating content. It establishes a static persona and is most effective when the task requires a specific level of expertise, seniority, or doctrinal depth.

> ***Example Prompt***
>
> *"You are a Senior Contract Attorney with twenty years of experience in cross-border technology licensing transactions. Draft a confidentiality clause for a technology licensing agreement between a United States licensor and a European licensee. Ensure full compliance with General Data Protection Regulation cross-border data transfer requirements."*

By specifying both the professional role and years of experience, the prompt signals the model to avoid explanatory simplifications and to employ precise legal terminology. Seniority cues tend to produce more conservative, risk-aware drafting, emphasizing compliance, foreseeability, and enforceability over brevity.

The "Role" technique is particularly effective for contract drafting, compliance documentation, internal memoranda, and other deliverables where doctrinal accuracy and professional tone are paramount.

The "Act As" Technique (Behavioral Prompting)

The "Act As" technique focuses on conduct rather than identity. It instructs the AI to perform a task in the manner of a particular professional actor, emphasizing strategy, tone, and situational judgment. This approach is especially valuable for dynamic or adversarial scenarios.

> ***Example Prompt***
>
> *"Act as a defense attorney preparing an opening statement for a complex fraud trial. Your objective is to humanize the defendant while methodically challenging the prosecution's burden of proof. Structure the argument logically, maintain professional decorum, and employ persuasive rhetoric appropriate for a jury audience."*

Here, the objective extends beyond legal correctness to encompass advocacy strategy and rhetorical framing. The "Act as" formulation activates the model's persuasive and stylistic capabilities, enabling practitioners to test arguments, rehearse positioning, and explore alternative narrative strategies before live proceedings.

This technique is well suited to negotiation simulations, courtroom advocacy preparation, client counseling scenarios, and strategic planning exercises.

The "Assume" Technique (Perspective-Based Prompting)

The "Assume" technique directs the AI to adopt a hypothetical or adversarial analytical position. It functions as a structured "what if" engine and is particularly effective for stress-testing legal arguments through adversarial review.

> ***Example Prompt***
> *"Assume the perspective of a conservative constitutional law scholar. Review the following argument concerning the legality of a government-mandated digital surveillance program. Critically assess potential conflicts with the Fourth Amendment and with international privacy norms."*

By instructing the AI to assume a specific ideological or professional stance, the model departs from its default neutral posture and delivers a sharper, more critical evaluation. This enables lawyers to identify weaknesses, anticipate counterarguments, and refine their reasoning before exposure to opposing counsel or judicial scrutiny.

The Assume technique is especially valuable for red teaming, appellate strategy, constitutional analysis, and comparative legal assessment.

Table 3.1 provides a concise comparison of the three role-based prompting techniques, outlining their conceptual focus, structural formulation, and optimal legal applications.

Table 3.1: Comparative Overview of Role-Based Prompting Techniques in Legal AI Practice.

Technique	Core Concept	Prompt Structure	Ideal Legal Application
"Role" Technique	Identity (Static)	*"You are a [specific expert]..."*	Contract drafting, due diligence, compliance memoranda
"Act As" Technique	Behavior (Dynamic)	*"Act as a [professional]* performing *[task]..."*	Negotiation simulations, litigation strategy, client role-play
"Assume" Technique	Perspective (Hypothetical)	*"Assume the position* of [adversary or analyst]..."	Red teaming, stress-testing arguments, comparative analysis.

Conclusion

Assigning roles is one of the most efficient methods for elevating AI-generated outputs from generic responses to professional-grade legal work product. Practitioners should begin with the "Role" technique for document-centric tasks requiring precision and doctrinal rigor, transition to "Act As" prompting for strategic or advocacy-driven exercises, and deploy "Assume" prompting when critically evaluating arguments from opposing perspectives.

When combined with advanced prompting methods—such as Chain-of-Thought reasoning or prompt chaining—role-based prompting transforms the Large Language Model from a passive drafting aid into a context-aware, analytically disciplined legal assistant.

14

Common Prompting Mistakes

Building on the foundational strategy of Assigning Roles in Legal Prompting, the next critical step is disciplined prompt construction. Even a well-defined role can be undermined by poorly structured instructions, resulting in inaccurate analysis, fabricated citations, logical gaps, or ethical exposure. Effective prompt engineering transforms a Large Language Model (LLM) from a generic conversational tool into a disciplined legal collaborator; flawed prompting does the opposite.

This chapter examines twelve common prompting mistakes, grouped into three categories: Structural Errors, Contextual Errors, and Professional and Ethical Errors. Each section identifies the risk, illustrates the error, and demonstrates a corrective approach consistent with professional legal standards.

I. Structural Errors (How the Prompt Is Written)

1. Vague or Ambiguous Prompts

Legal prompts demand precision. Ambiguous instructions force the model to infer missing details, often resulting in generic or irrelevant output. In legal work, such imprecision can materially distort analysis.

Vague Prompt Example

"Write a legal document about a contract dispute."

This prompt fails to specify the nature of the dispute, the type of document, the governing law, or the desired remedy, compelling the AI to guess the legal context.

Improved Prompt Example

"Draft a complaint for breach of contract arising from a business partnership dispute under California law. Seek damages for lost profits and include relevant statutory authority."

This version clearly defines the legal issue, document type, jurisdiction, and objective, enabling a focused and legally appropriate response.

2. Overly Complicated or Excessively Long Prompts

Prompts that attempt to cover too many issues simultaneously overwhelm the model, leading to fragmented or superficial responses. Legal prompting benefits from prioritization, not exhaustiveness.

> ***Overly Complicated Prompt Example***
>
> *"Imagine you are a corporate lawyer drafting a comprehensive joint venture agreement covering profit sharing, intellectual property, dispute resolution, employment terms, confidentiality, indemnification, exit strategies, penalties, arbitration provisions, and all other necessary clauses."*

This prompt includes too many competing instructions and undefined expectations ("all other necessary clauses"), making it difficult for the AI to generate coherent output.

> ***Improved Prompt Example***
>
> *"Draft key provisions of a joint venture agreement focusing on profit sharing, intellectual property ownership, and dispute resolution mechanisms."*

This narrowed focus produces usable content that can later be expanded through iterative prompting.

3. Inconsistent or Contradictory Instructions

Contradictory prompts create logical dead ends. Internal consistency is essential, particularly in legal analysis and drafting.

> ***Inconsistent Prompt Example***
>
> *"Write a memorandum explaining tenants' rights under a residential lease, assuming the tenant has no lease but is entitled to lease-based protections."*

This prompt simultaneously denies and affirms the existence of a lease, forcing the AI to resolve the contradiction rather than perform the task.

> ***Consistent Prompt Example***
>
> *"Write a legal memorandum explaining tenants' rights under a written residential lease, with particular emphasis on eviction protections under New York City law."*

The revised prompt establishes a coherent legal premise and jurisdiction.

4. Overloading a Single Prompt with Multiple Tasks

Combining multiple analytical objectives into one prompt often produces disorganized results. Complex legal workflows should be broken into sequential steps.

Overloaded Prompt Example

Write a legal opinion on negligence in a car accident case, including liability analysis, defenses, statutes, damages, case law, outcomes, and recommendations."

This prompt demands several distinct outputs that are better handled separately.

Focused Prompt Example

"Analyze whether the defendant in a car accident case can successfully assert contributory negligence as a defense."

This approach enables depth, clarity, and analytical rigor.

II. Contextual Errors (What the Prompt Omits)

5. Insufficient Legal Context

Legal prompting requires sufficient contextual framing to anchor the model's analysis in the correct doctrinal and jurisdictional setting. When essential details such as the applicable area of law, governing jurisdiction, or legal issue are omitted, the model defaults to high-level generalities that lack practical legal value.

Prompt Lacking Context

"Write a legal brief about intellectual property."

This prompt is overly broad and fails to specify the relevant intellectual property regime, the legal question at issue, or the governing jurisdiction. As a result, the AI is forced to generalize across multiple doctrinal areas, producing a descriptive overview rather than a focused legal argument.

Improved Prompt with Sufficient Context

"Write a legal brief analyzing the enforceability of a trademark registration under United States law, focusing on distinctiveness requirements and challenges posed by prior similar trademarks."

This version narrows the scope to trademark law, defines the legal issue, and identifies the jurisdiction, enabling the AI to generate a targeted analysis grounded in specific statutory and jurisprudential standards.

6. Ignoring Legal Terminology or Jargon

Legal drafting depends on precise terminology that reflects statutory language and procedural requirements. Prompts that rely on informal or non-technical phrasing often yield outputs that lack the formality and legal sufficiency required in professional practice.

Prompt Lacking Legal Terminology

"Write a letter telling a tenant they are being evicted."

This prompt reduces a legally regulated process to an informal communication task, omitting statutory references, notice requirements, and procedural safeguards. The resulting output risks being legally inadequate or unenforceable.

Legally Precise Prompt Example

"Draft an eviction notice under California's unlawful detainer statute, specifying the grounds for termination and the statutory timeframe to cure the breach or vacate."

By incorporating precise legal terminology and statutory grounding, this prompt guides the AI to produce a document consistent with professional landlord–tenant practice.

7. Not Accounting for Updates or Changes in the Law

Laws are dynamic. Failing to specify the need for current information can lead to outdated or inaccurate responses, especially when dealing with recent legislation.

Outdated Prompt Example

"Write a summary of U.K. corporate mergers and acquisitions law."

This prompt does not specify that the information must reflect the most recent legal developments, which could result in the AI using older, pre-reform statutory information.

Example Prompt Accounting for Updates

"Write a summary of current U.K. corporate mergers and acquisitions laws, including recent changes under the 2024 Merger Reform Act."

This explicit instruction ensures the AI generates content that is both relevant and timely, reflecting the most up-to-date legal environment.

8. Failure to Specify the Intended Audience

The complexity and tone of a legal response must be tailored to the audience (e.g., senior partner vs. non-expert client). Failing to specify the audience results in miscommunication.

Prompt Lacking Audience Specification

"Write a memo on patent infringement."

The response will default to a technical, academic tone which may be too complex for a client or too basic for a patent attorney.

Prompt With Audience Specification

"Write a legal memo on patent infringement for a client with limited legal knowledge, explaining potential consequences in simple terms."

This clarifies that the audience is a non-expert, guiding the AI to use accessible language and practical explanations while maintaining professional authority.

III. Professional and Ethical Errors (Risks)

9. Biased or Leading Prompts

In legal contexts, prompts that suggest a specific outcome or viewpoint lead to biased responses that merely confirm the user's belief rather than analyzing the law impartially.

Biased Prompt Example

"Write a persuasive argument defending the client in a personal injury case where the defendant was clearly negligent and caused significant harm."

The prompt assumes guilt, directing the AI toward a biased defense, which undermines objective legal analysis and the duty to assess risk fairly.

Neutral Prompt Example

"Write an objective analysis of the plaintiff's claim, but dedicate a section to formulating a persuasive argument for the defendant based on contributory negligence."

This version requires the AI to perform a balanced analysis and generate a defensible argument based on legal principles, not pre-assumed facts.

Unrealistic Expectations of AI Capabilities

AI cannot replace thorough legal analysis, expert judgment, or evidence review. Prompts must request achievable summaries or drafts, not full strategic execution.

Unrealistic Prompt Example

"Write a full legal defense for a complex multi-million-dollar class action securities fraud lawsuit, including legal research, evidence review, and strategy recommendations."

This prompt asks the AI to provide a level of strategic depth and evidence review that exceeds its current capabilities, likely yielding a generalized or inaccurate strategy.

Realistic Prompt Example

"Summarize potential legal defenses in a securities fraud case based on U.S. federal law and recent case law."

This prompt requests a more achievable output (a synthesis of defenses), enabling the lawyer to use the AI's summary as a starting point for specialized strategic work.

10. Failure to Mandate Citation and Fact-Checking

Large Language Models are prone to hallucination (fabricating facts or citations). Failure to explicitly mandate verifiable sources is a critical ethical and professional liability.

Prompt Without Citation Mandate

"Analyze the application of 'duty of care' to autonomous vehicle manufacturers."

With this prompt, the AI may generate plausible but entirely fabricated case law or misinterpret existing statutes, exposing the user to citation fraud risk.

Prompt with Mandating Citation

"Analyze the application of 'duty of care' to autonomous vehicle manufacturers. All analysis must be supported by footnotes referencing specific, verifiable case law and statute citations."

This prompt enforces academic and professional rigor, forcing the AI to focus on grounded information and providing an immediate check for the user.

11. Breaching Ethical and Confidentiality Obligation

Professional responsibility rules prohibit disclosure of identifiable client information to unsecured third-party systems. Prompts must abstract sensitive facts.

Ethically Unsound Prompt

"Analyze confidential client Kojo Dawson's financial audit for liability under the Sarbanes–Oxley Act."

This prompt exposes privileged client information to an external system.

Ethically Sound Prompt

"Assume a hypothetical financial audit involving three defined compliance risk factors. Analyze potential liability under the Sarbanes–Oxley Act."

By abstracting client-specific data, this prompt preserves confidentiality while enabling legal analysis.

Conclusion

The effectiveness of AI in legal practice depends directly on the rigor of prompt engineering. The twelve mistakes outlined here—from ambiguity and complexity to failing ethical safeguards—represent core friction points between human legal reasoning and machine output. Avoiding these pitfalls demands precision, impartiality, and ethical vigilance. By applying robust prompt structures, mandating external verification, and abstracting privileged information, legal professionals transform AI from a source of liability into a reliable collaborator, enhancing the integrity and depth of their work.

Part IV

Crafting Effective Prompts for Specific Legal Tasks

Crafting effective prompts for specific legal tasks requires more than technical familiarity with artificial intelligence systems; it demands a disciplined understanding of legal reasoning, professional standards, and the operational behavior of Large Language Models (LLMs). Legal practitioners must learn to articulate instructions that guide AI tools—whether general-purpose models such as ChatGPT and Gemini or specialized platforms such as CoCounsel—toward outputs that are accurate, context-aware, and jurisdictionally compliant.

Each category of legal work—research, drafting, compliance, litigation support, policy analysis, or client communication—presents distinct objectives, risks, and constraints. A prompt that performs well for summarization may be unsuitable for compliance review or litigation analysis. Consequently, effective prompting is inherently task-specific. The quality and reliability of AI-generated output depend entirely on how clearly the prompt defines its purpose, scope, legal context, audience, and constraints.

This chapter presents a structured framework for crafting effective prompts across core legal functions. Each section explains the nature of the task, identifies the essential components of a well-formed prompt, and provides a professionally grounded example with explanatory commentary.

Legal Research Prompts

Legal research underpins competent legal advice and sound advocacy. AI-assisted research prompts can significantly reduce time spent retrieving authorities and synthesizing doctrinal trends. However, absent precise instructions, AI systems tend to produce broad overviews rather than legally actionable analysis. Precision is therefore essential to minimize hallucination risk and ensure professional utility.

Crafting Effective Legal Research Prompts

An effective research prompt should clearly articulate the research objective (such as identifying precedent, interpreting statutes, or analyzing doctrinal principles), specify the jurisdiction and subject area, define the desired output format, and impose constraints regarding recency, authority level, or citation requirements.

> ***Example Prompt***
>
> *"Act as a legal researcher. Identify three post-2020 judicial precedents addressing wrongful termination under United Kingdom employment law. Provide the case names, official citations, and a 200-word analytical summary of each decision's legal reasoning."*

This prompt combines role assignment with clearly defined jurisdictional and temporal boundaries. By specifying both the form and substance of the output—

including word limits and citation expectations—it ensures that the response integrates smoothly into professional research workflows and remains verifiable.

Contract Drafting Prompts

Contract drafting demands doctrinal accuracy, linguistic precision, and regulatory awareness. When properly instructed, LLMs can efficiently generate draft clauses or suggest alternative formulations that reflect standard market practice. However, vague drafting prompts often omit critical compliance considerations or fail to reflect the parties' legal relationship.

Crafting Effective Contract Drafting Prompts

Effective drafting prompts identify the contract type, define the parties and governing law, isolate the specific clause or section to be drafted, and impose constraints relating to tone, length, or regulatory compliance.

> ***Example Prompt***
> *"Act as a commercial lawyer. Draft a confidentiality clause for a cross-border technology licensing agreement between a United States licensor and a European software developer. Ensure strict compliance with the General Data Protection Regulation concerning international data transfers."*

By explicitly referencing the cross-border nature of the transaction and applicable data protection law, this prompt directs the AI to incorporate compliance-sensitive language that would otherwise be omitted in a generic drafting request.

Legal Compliance Prompts

Compliance analysis requires systematic identification of regulatory gaps and risk exposure. AI-assisted compliance prompts function best when framed as structured review exercises rather than open-ended commentary. When properly designed, they can operate as an initial screening mechanism for policies, contracts, or internal procedures.

Crafting Effective Compliance Prompts

Effective compliance prompts identify the regulatory framework, specify the document under review, instruct the AI to flag deficiencies or risks, and require structured output for ease of review.

> ***Example Prompt***
>
> *"Review the privacy policy text provided below. Identify compliance gaps specifically relating to the General Data Protection Regulation and the California Consumer Privacy Act. Present the findings in a two-column table, listing the detected issue and a recommended revision."*

Requiring a tabular format forces analytical discipline and transforms narrative critique into an actionable compliance checklist suitable for legal and operational teams.

Legal Summarization Prompts

Summarization assists legal professionals in extracting core principles from lengthy judgments, contracts, or evidentiary records. Without careful guidance, AI-generated summaries often overemphasize procedural detail at the expense of doctrinal significance.

Crafting Effective Summarization Prompts

Effective summarization prompts specify the document type, define the analytical focus, and impose constraints regarding length and tone.

> ***Example Prompt***
> *"Summarize the judgment in Donoghue v Stevenson (1932). Focus exclusively on the material facts, the articulation of the duty of care principle, and its significance in the development of tort law. Limit the summary to 250 words."*

By directing attention to substantive legal reasoning rather than historical narrative, this prompt ensures an academically precise and professionally useful summary.

Client Communication Prompts

Client communication requires clarity, empathy, and ethical restraint. AI-assisted drafting can help translate complex legal concepts into accessible language, but prompts must explicitly guide tone and audience sensitivity to avoid miscommunication or unrealistic assurances.

Crafting Effective Client Communication Prompts

Effective prompts define the communication purpose, specify the intended audience, establish tone, and impose ethical constraints—particularly regarding guarantees or outcomes.

> ***Example Prompt***
> *"Act as a senior legal advisor. Draft a concise email explaining to a client why their negligence claim may not succeed under United Kingdom law. Use plain language appropriate for a non-expert audience and maintain a professional, empathetic tone."*

This prompt ensures that the AI's output supports client understanding while preserving professional boundaries and managing expectations.

Litigation Support Prompts

Litigation support tasks include organizing evidence, constructing timelines, and identifying factual inconsistencies. AI systems are particularly effective in processing large volumes of text to detect patterns, provided the prompt clearly defines the litigation stage and analytical task.

Crafting Effective Litigation Support Prompts

Effective prompts identify the procedural context, specify the analytical task, reference the relevant materials, and define the desired output format.

> ***Example Prompt***
> *"Act as a litigation support assistant. Analyze the provided witness statements and produce a chronological timeline of events relevant to this breach of contract dispute. Highlight any material inconsistencies between the witnesses' accounts."*

This prompt leverages the model's capacity for comparative textual analysis, producing a structured foundation that legal teams can verify and refine.

Legal Policy Analysis Prompts

Policy analysis requires synthesis across legal, ethical, and economic dimensions. AI-assisted prompts can support comparative analysis and scenario modeling when properly constrained and contextualized.

Crafting Effective Legal Policy Analysis Prompts

Effective policy prompts identify the policy domain, define the analytical objective, specify the jurisdiction, and reference applicable frameworks or standards.

> ***Example Prompt***
> *"Act as a legal policy analyst. Evaluate the potential impact of adopting a national artificial intelligence governance framework in Ghana modeled on the European Union Artificial Intelligence Act. Discuss the legal, ethical, and economic implications in a 400-word policy brief."*

This prompt directs the AI to deliver multidimensional analysis suitable for legislative or regulatory consideration, while remaining within defined analytical bounds.

Conclusion

Effective legal prompting is an exercise in strategic clarity. Across research, drafting, compliance, litigation, and policy analysis, the reliability of AI-generated output depends entirely on the precision with which legal objectives, context, and constraints are articulated. Poorly framed prompts invite ambiguity and risk; well-designed prompts transform AI systems into disciplined analytical tools.

Part V

Evaluating and Refining AI Outputs

The capacity to critically evaluate and refine AI-generated outputs is a core professional competency for the modern legal practitioner. Although tools such as ChatGPT, Gemini, and CoCounsel can rapidly generate legal summaries, draft arguments, or preliminary documents, their outputs do not possess intrinsic authority. The reliability and professional value of AI-assisted work depend entirely on rigorous human oversight.

Evaluation ensures that AI-generated content conforms to legal accuracy, ethical obligations, and contextual relevance. Without disciplined review, risks such as hallucinated authorities, inaccurate statutory references, or jurisdictional misalignment may compromise professional credibility and expose practitioners to liability. Refinement, therefore, is not a superficial editorial exercise; it is the mechanism through which professional accountability is preserved within AI-assisted legal workflows.

Purpose and Benefits of Evaluating AI Outputs

Systematic evaluation of AI-generated legal content serves several strategic functions within professional practice. First, it ensures factual and doctrinal accuracy by confirming that cited statutes, cases, and legal interpretations align with authoritative sources. Second, it mitigates professional risk by preventing blind reliance on erroneous or fabricated output. Third, it supports quality control by maintaining consistency with firm standards, jurisdictional requirements, and stylistic conventions. Finally, it enhances efficiency by informing prompt refinement, allowing subsequent interactions with the model to produce more targeted and reliable results.

In this sense, evaluation bridges the gap between automation and legal expertise. It ensures that artificial intelligence functions as a controlled analytical aid rather than a substitute for professional judgment.

The Five-Step Evaluation Protocol

To maintain consistency and reliability, legal professionals should apply a structured evaluation protocol to all AI-generated outputs, regardless of task or platform.

Step One: Source Verification (The Reality Check)

Every factual assertion, statutory reference, or judicial citation generated by an AI system must be independently verified against authoritative legal sources.

This step is non-negotiable in professional practice. If an AI-generated summary refers to a specific statutory provision or case, the practitioner must confirm its existence, accuracy, and current validity using trusted databases such as Lexis+, Westlaw, official law reports, or government repositories.

This verification process guards against hallucinated authorities and ensures that reliance is placed only on verifiable legal sources.

Step Two: Contextual and Jurisdictional Review

AI systems often draw on global training data and may inadvertently blend authorities from different jurisdictions. Legal professionals must therefore assess whether the output is appropriately confined to the intended legal system and procedural context. When preparing jurisdiction-specific analysis, it is essential to confirm that cited cases, statutes, and doctrinal principles originate from the correct legal framework.

This step is particularly critical in cross-border matters, comparative analysis, and regulatory compliance work, where jurisdictional precision is fundamental.

Step Three: Logical and Structural Assessment

Beyond factual accuracy, AI-generated content must be evaluated for logical coherence and doctrinal structure. Legal reasoning should follow established analytical frameworks—such as Issue, Rule, Application, and Conclusion (IRAC)—without unsupported assumptions or logical leaps. Practitioners should scrutinize whether the conclusions drawn are adequately supported by the premises and whether counterarguments or limitations have been appropriately acknowledged.

This assessment ensures that AI outputs reflect sound legal reasoning rather than superficially persuasive narratives.

Step Four: Ethical and Confidentiality Review

AI-generated content must be examined for compliance with professional responsibility and data protection obligations. Practitioners should ensure that the output does not disclose confidential or privileged information, propose unethical strategies, or misrepresent legal certainty. In regulated environments, this review also includes verifying compliance with applicable professional rules and data protection regimes, such as the General Data Protection Regulation or relevant professional conduct standards.

Ethical review reinforces the principle that responsibility for AI-assisted work remains with the human practitioner.

Step Five: Language, Tone, and Professional Style Review

Finally, AI-generated text must be assessed for linguistic precision and professional tone. AI systems frequently default to an informal or advisory style that may be inappropriate for legal documents. Practitioners should refine language to ensure neutrality, formality, and doctrinal clarity, eliminating speculative phrasing, conversational expressions, or overconfident assertions unsupported by authority.

This step ensures that the final output meets professional drafting standards and is suitable for its intended audience.

Refining AI Outputs Through Iterative Design

Refinement is an iterative process in which practitioners actively engage with the AI system to improve clarity, depth, and structure. Rather than accepting initial outputs at face value, legal professionals should use targeted follow-up prompts to address ambiguities, expand analysis, or reformat content.

Clarification prompts can be used to unpack reasoning or explain the basis of specific conclusions. Depth can be adjusted by instructing the model to incorporate additional authorities or comparative perspectives. Formatting refinements may require the AI to reorganize content into memoranda, tables, or structured checklists that align with professional workflows.

Illustrative Refinement Loop

An initial prompt requesting a summary of the General Data Protection Regulation's impact on cross-border data transfers may yield a broadly accurate but incomplete response. Upon review, the practitioner may identify omissions relating to recent jurisprudence or regulatory developments. A refinement prompt that explicitly requests inclusion of the *Schrems II* decision and subsequent regulatory frameworks transforms the output from a general overview into a current, practice-ready analysis.

This iterative process demonstrates how disciplined refinement elevates AI-generated content from generic exposition to professional-grade legal analysis.

Structured Evaluation Framework

To support consistency, practitioners may employ an evaluation matrix that aligns accuracy, context, logic, ethics, and language with corresponding refinement techniques. Such frameworks provide a systematic approach to reviewing AI outputs and ensure that no critical dimension of professional quality control is overlooked.

Best Practices for Evaluating and Refining AI Output

Effective use of AI in legal practice is grounded in disciplined habits. Legal professionals should consistently verify AI-generated content against authoritative sources, treat initial outputs as drafts rather than conclusions, and maintain documentation of prompts and revisions to support accountability. Cross-checking complex issues across multiple tools further reduces risk, while incorporating corrections within ongoing sessions improves model responsiveness and output quality.

Conclusion

Evaluating and refining AI-generated output is not an optional enhancement; it is an essential discipline in AI-assisted legal practice. Through systematic verification, contextual review, ethical oversight, and iterative refinement, legal professionals transform raw AI responses into reliable, jurisdictionally sound, and professionally defensible work product.

When human judgment remains central, artificial intelligence becomes a powerful analytical partner—enhancing efficiency and insight without compromising the integrity, responsibility, or credibility of the legal profession.

17

Legal Accuracy vs. AI Hallucination

One of the most consequential distinctions in AI-assisted legal practice lies between ***legal accuracy** and **AI hallucination***. Legal accuracy denotes the factual, procedural, and contextual correctness of an AI-generated output—ensuring that every citation, precedent, statutory reference, and analytical conclusion is grounded in verifiable legal authority.

By contrast, ***AI hallucination*** occurs when a system produces information that is linguistically plausible yet legally false. This may include fabricated case names, incorrect statutory provisions, misattributed judicial reasoning, or invented legal principles. Although such outputs often resemble competent legal writing in tone and structure, their adoption without verification poses serious ethical, professional, and reputational risks.

Understanding this distinction is essential. In legal practice, credibility is inseparable from accuracy, and even a single unverified reference can undermine an otherwise sound argument.

Understanding Legal Accuracy in AI Outputs

In the legal domain, accuracy extends well beyond grammatical precision or stylistic fluency. It rests on three interdependent pillars.

1. **Authority verification** requires confirming that all cited statutes, cases, regulations, and secondary sources actually exist and are referenced correctly. This includes accurate party names, dates, jurisdictions, and reporter citations.

2. **Contextual alignment** ensures that legal analysis corresponds to the correct jurisdiction, procedural posture, and factual setting. For example, citing United Kingdom case law in support of a United States contract dispute—unless expressly framed as comparative analysis—constitutes a substantive legal error.

3. **Reasoning consistency** demands that the logical structure of the analysis conforms to accepted legal methodologies, such as statutory interpretation principles or issue–rule–application–conclusion reasoning. Even where authorities are real, flawed reasoning can render an output professionally unreliable.

Consider an AI-generated reference to *Smith v. Green (2019)*. Before incorporating such a citation, the legal professional must verify its existence in an authoritative database. A disciplined approach may include re-prompting the system with a verification instruction, such as:

"Verify whether Smith v. Green (2019) exists in a recognized jurisdiction. If the case cannot be confirmed, state that explicitly."

This practice reinforces accuracy while exposing uncertainty rather than concealing it behind confident language.

Recognizing AI Hallucination

AI hallucinations most commonly arise from incomplete prompts, ambiguous instructions, or gaps in the model's training data. Because large language models are designed to generate statistically plausible continuations of text, they may "fill in" missing information with fabricated yet convincing content.

Hallucinations typically manifest in several recurring forms. Nonexistent citations often appear as cases with credible-sounding party names and dates but no traceable record. Phantom statutes may involve invented section numbers or mischaracterized provisions of otherwise real legislation. Misattributed quotations can assign authentic legal principles to the wrong judge, court, or decision.

A particularly dangerous aspect of hallucination is what may be described as the *plausibility trap*. A sentence such as, *"According to Johnson v. California (2022), contract terms may be reinterpreted where commercial fairness demands it,"* may read as authoritative. Yet if the cited case cannot be located in any official reporter or court archive, the reference is legally meaningless—regardless of how persuasive the prose appears.

Mitigating Hallucination and Reinforcing Accuracy

Preventing hallucination is not achieved through passive reliance on AI tools but through active and systematic safeguards. Legal professionals should consistently cross-check all citations against authoritative databases, including official court websites, government portals, and trusted legal research platforms.

Prompt design also plays a critical role. Constraining instructions—for example, directing the model to include only cases verifiable through official judicial sources—significantly reduces the likelihood of fabricated authorities. Iterative validation further strengthens reliability by requiring the model to supply specific reporter citations or publicly accessible references for each legal authority mentioned.

Above all, human oversight remains indispensable. Lawyers must personally assess jurisdictional relevance, analytical coherence, and ethical compliance. AI may assist in drafting or research, but it cannot assume responsibility for legal judgment.

Conclusion

The line between effective AI assistance and professional negligence is often drawn by the user's vigilance. Legal accuracy is not secured by the confidence with which an AI presents its output but by the rigor with which that output is verified. By maintaining disciplined review practices and embedding accuracy checks into AI-assisted workflows, legal professionals ensure that artificial intelligence remains a valuable collaborator rather than a source of misinformation.

18

Verification and Validation Protocols

Verification and validation function as the twin safeguards of AI-assisted legal practice. Together, they ensure that AI-generated outputs meet the standards of factual accuracy, logical coherence, and professional reliability required of legal work.

Verification addresses factual integrity by asking whether a cited case, statute, or authority actually exists and is accurately referenced. **Validation**, by contrast, evaluates analytical soundness by examining whether the identified authorities have been applied correctly within the relevant legal and jurisdictional context. These processes are not optional technical checks; they are professional obligations grounded in the ethical duties of competence, diligence, and accuracy.

By systematically applying both protocols, legal professionals prevent inadvertent reliance on fabricated, outdated, or contextually inappropriate material.

Verification Protocols: The Fact-Checking Discipline

Verification ensures that all legal references produced by an AI system are authentic and traceable. Every cited statute, regulation, or judicial decision must be cross-checked against authoritative legal sources, including official court repositories, government publications, or established legal research platforms.

A practical verification strategy involves compelling the model to disclose the basis of its claims. When access to premium databases is unavailable, structured prompting becomes especially important. For example, a "show your work" instruction requires the system to enumerate the legal authorities supporting its analysis and identify where those authorities may be found. A prompt such as:

> *"List the specific statutes and judicial precedents supporting this analysis, and indicate the source or retrieval location for each,"*

forces transparency and exposes uncertainty rather than masking it behind confident prose.

Another effective technique is *parallel querying,* in which the same legal question is posed to more than one model. When different systems produce inconsistent authorities or conflicting references, this divergence signals the need for immediate manual verification. Agreement between models does not guarantee accuracy, but inconsistency is a strong indicator of potential error.

Validation Protocols: The Logic and Context Review

Validation focuses on whether the reasoning itself is legally sound and contextually appropriate. A frequent failure in AI-generated legal analysis occurs when a correct authority is identified but misapplied to a legal issue beyond its intended scope. For instance, a criminal statute may be accurately cited yet incorrectly invoked in a civil dispute, or an employment law principle may be applied without regard to worker classification.

Contextual validation can be achieved through targeted follow-up prompts that test the robustness of the analysis. Asking whether the reasoning aligns with current precedent in a specified jurisdiction, or whether the conclusion would change under a different factual assumption, helps surface hidden flaws. A prompt such as:

> *"Assess whether this reasoning is consistent with current employment law precedent in [specified jurisdiction]. Would the conclusion differ if the worker were classified as an independent contractor?"*

invites the model to re-examine its analytical boundaries.

Self-correction prompts further strengthen validation by requiring the AI to articulate its reasoning process. Instructing the system to summarize the logical steps leading to its conclusion and to identify any assumptions made often reveals gaps, overgeneralizations, or unsupported inferences that require human correction.

Verification in the Absence of Premium Databases

For practitioners without access to subscription-based legal research platforms, disciplined prompting and manual cross-checking become essential safeguards. Source-constrained prompts that limit references to official government or judicial websites significantly reduce the likelihood of hallucinated authorities. For example:

> *"Provide only information that can be verified on official government or judiciary websites."*

The citations generated through such prompts can then be used as search queries in publicly accessible resources, including Google Scholar and national court repositories such as the British and Irish Legal Information Institute (BAILII) or the Canadian Legal Information Institute (CanLII). This approach transforms AI output into a starting point for verification rather than a substitute for it.

Conclusion

Verification establishes what is factually true; validation explains why and how it is legally relevant. Together, they form a continuous, cyclical process of review and refinement that underpins responsible AI-assisted lawyering. By embedding verification and validation protocols into everyday workflows, legal professionals uphold the standards of diligence, accuracy, and professional judgment that define the practice of law—even in an age of advanced automation.

19

Bias Mitigation and Transparency

As artificial intelligence becomes embedded in legal workflows, two interdependent ethical imperatives rise to the forefront: ***bias mitigation***, which seeks to prevent prejudiced or one-sided reasoning, and ***transparency***, which ensures that AI-generated analysis is intelligible, traceable, and open to professional scrutiny. Together, these principles form the ethical backbone of responsible AI adoption in legal practice.

Without deliberate safeguards, AI systems risk reinforcing inequities or obscuring the reasoning behind their outputs. Legal professionals must therefore engage proactively with both concerns, treating them as ongoing responsibilities rather than one-time technical adjustments.

Understanding Bias in Legal AI

Bias in AI-generated legal outputs generally arises from three identifiable sources.

The first is ***training data bias***. Large Language Models are trained on extensive corpora of publicly available text, much of which reflects historical social inequalities, dominant legal traditions, or an overrepresentation of Western—particularly United States—legal materials. Without corrective instruction, this imbalance can skew legal analysis toward certain jurisdictions or normative assumptions.

The second source is ***prompt design bias***. The way a question is framed can predetermine the model's analytical direction. For example, a prompt that asks, "Why is the defendant guilty?" implicitly assumes culpability and compels the system to construct an argument that ignores exculpatory facts or alternative interpretations. In such cases, bias is introduced not by the model itself, but by the user's framing.

The third source is ***interpretive bias***. Even when prompts are neutrally phrased, AI systems may default to familiar jurisprudential frameworks, such as common law reasoning, unless explicitly instructed to apply alternative legal traditions. This tendency can marginalize civil law systems, customary law, or hybrid legal regimes, particularly in non-Western jurisdictions.

Bias Mitigation Protocols

Mitigating bias requires intentional, bias-aware prompt design and structured analytical demands. One foundational strategy is ***neutral framing***, which avoids presupposed conclusions and invites balanced assessment. A prompt that assigns fault in advance narrows the analytical space, whereas a prompt that asks for an examination of competing liabilities preserves objectivity and legal rigor.

A second strategy is ***multi-perspective prompting***. By explicitly requesting contrasting interpretations—such as *"arguments supporting both plaintiff and* *defendant"*—the legal professional compels the AI to engage in adversarial reasoning rather than advocacy for a single position. This approach mirrors traditional legal analysis and reduces the risk of one-sided conclusions.

A third and particularly critical strategy is ***jurisdictional specificity***. Because training data may disproportionately reflect certain legal systems, prompts should explicitly identify the applicable legal tradition and instruct the model not to default to more dominant frameworks. Directing the AI to analyze an issue under a specific customary, civil, or hybrid legal system helps counter structural imbalances embedded in training data.

Transparency in AI Reasoning

Transparency addresses a distinct but related concern: the opacity of AI-generated conclusions. Large Language Models operate on probabilistic pattern recognition rather than legal understanding. As a result, lawyers must actively demand visibility into the reasoning process that produces a given output.

Traceability prompts serve this function by requiring the model to articulate the logical steps underlying its conclusion and to identify any assumptions made along the way. This transforms the output from a declarative answer into an analyzable reasoning chain that can be evaluated, challenged, and refined.

Confidence calibration further enhances transparency. Asking the model to assign a confidence level to its analysis and to indicate whether the conclusion rests on settled law or novel interpretation helps the user distinguish between well-established doctrine and speculative reasoning. This distinction is particularly important when AI-generated content is used in advisory, policy, or risk-assessment contexts.

Conclusion

Bias mitigation and transparency are not ancillary considerations; they are structural foundations of ethical AI use in legal practice. By consciously identifying potential sources of bias and insisting on explainable reasoning, legal professionals preserve the integrity of their analysis and the credibility of AI-assisted work.

When these principles are consistently applied, artificial intelligence ceases to function as an opaque "black box" and instead becomes an accountable, scrutinizable collaborator—one whose contributions can be tested, validated, and responsibly integrated into professional legal judgment.

20

Ethical and Confidentiality Safeguards

Ethical integrity remains the cornerstone of legal practice. The integration of artificial intelligence into legal workflows introduces distinct vulnerabilities, including the inadvertent disclosure of privileged information, overreliance on unverified outputs, and breaches of confidentiality obligations. Addressing these risks requires intentional, structured safeguards grounded in established principles of professional responsibility.

AI tools do not diminish ethical duties; rather, they amplify the need for vigilance. Lawyers must therefore approach AI use not as a technical convenience, but as an extension of their fiduciary obligations to clients, courts, and the legal system. The following five principles outline the core ethical and confidentiality obligations that govern responsible AI use in legal practice.

1. Maintaining Client Confidentiality through Anonymization

The protection of client confidentiality is non-negotiable. Legal professionals must never input personally identifiable information or privileged client data into public or unsecured Large Language Models.

A core safeguard is ***abstraction***. Real names, case identifiers, financial figures, and proprietary facts should be replaced with neutral placeholders such as "Client A," "Company X," or "Hypothetical Scenario." This approach preserves analytical utility while eliminating the risk of exposing sensitive information.

For example, a prompt that references a named individual and a specific monetary dispute risks breaching confidentiality. By contrast, reframing the same task in hypothetical terms enables the AI to assist with legal structure and reasoning without accessing or retaining privileged facts. Abstraction is therefore not a limitation on AI use, but a prerequisite for ethical deployment.

2. Ethical Data Handling and Platform Selection

Beyond prompt design, ethical AI use requires scrutiny of how tools handle data. Legal professionals must understand and evaluate the data retention and training policies of any AI platform they employ.

Public, consumer-facing models often reserve the right to store or reuse inputs for model improvement. Such platforms are categorically inappropriate for client-related legal work. In contrast, enterprise-grade legal AI systems typically offer contractual assurances of zero data retention, restricted access, and enhanced security controls. These protections constitute the minimum acceptable standard for professional legal practice.

Selecting an AI tool is therefore an ethical decision as much as a technical one. Failure to assess data handling policies exposes lawyers to confidentiality breaches and potential professional misconduct.

Copyrighted Material

3. Professional Responsibility and the "Assistant" Principle

Artificial intelligence functions solely as an assistant, not as an authority. The lawyer retains full professional responsibility for every document drafted, argument advanced, or filing submitted with AI assistance.

This principle imposes an affirmative duty to verify. Submitting AI-generated content containing fabricated citations, misapplied statutes, or unsupported conclusions constitutes a breach of professional competence and diligence. Every AI output must be treated as a preliminary draft, subject to rigorous human review, verification, and revision.

Delegation to AI does not dilute accountability; it concentrates it.

4. Avoiding Conflicts of Interestand Data Leakage

Another ethical risk arises from potential data leakage. In non-secure or shared environments, there is a theoretical risk that proprietary strategies, drafting styles, or internal analyses could be learned and reproduced for other users.

To mitigate this risk, legal practitioners should rely exclusively on closed or private-instance AI systems that do not share training data across organizations or user groups. These systems preserve strategic confidentiality and prevent inadvertent cross-client contamination of legal reasoning or litigation strategy.

5. Transparency with Clients

Transparency is an essential component of trust. Where AI materially influences legal analysis, drafting, or billing practices, lawyers should be prepared to disclose its use in a clear and measured manner.

A carefully framed disclosure, emphasizing professional supervision, confidentiality safeguards, and human oversight, reinforces client confidence rather than undermining it. Transparency in this context is not an admission of delegation, but a demonstration of responsible innovation.

Conclusion

Ethical and confidentiality safeguards are not optional enhancements; they are foundational requirements of AI-assisted legal practice. Through disciplined anonymization, careful platform selection, rigorous verification, and transparent client communication, legal professionals can harness the benefits of AI without compromising their fiduciary duties.

When these safeguards are consistently applied, artificial intelligence becomes a trustworthy ally, one that enhances efficiency and insight while preserving the ethical standards upon which the legal profession is built.

Part VI

Prompt Packs for Legal Specialties

Across the earlier chapters, you explored the technological foundations of Artificial Intelligence, mastered core prompt-engineering techniques, and established verification protocols aligned with professional ethics and compliance standards. Together, these sections provided the analytical framework required to deploy generative AI safely, responsibly, and effectively within legal practice.

Now, the focus shifts from theory to implementation.

Part VI serves as a desk-side reference library of practical "Prompt Packs" created for specific legal specialties. These packs are not academic exercises; they are field-tested templates structured around the real workflows, regulatory demands, and time pressures lawyers face daily. Whether you are preparing for contentious depositions, conducting complex transactional due diligence, drafting regulatory disclosures, or managing compliance risk assessments, each pack provides immediately deployable starting points calibrated to your professional environment.

By integrating the advanced prompt-design techniques introduced in Part III with the validation and risk-control protocols presented in Part V, these Prompt Packs transform generative AI from a general research assistant into a task-specific professional support tool. Used correctly, they enable faster issue identification, clearer drafting, and more disciplined analysis—while firmly preserving the lawyer's central role as interpreter, advocate, and decision-maker.

Each Prompt Pack includes scenario framing, platform-specific workflow guidance, and adaptable templates designed for direct incorporation into daily legal practice.

Note: *Throughout this book, representative AI platforms are referenced to illustrate practical, real-world workflows. These examples do not constitute endorsements, and functionally equivalent tools may be used to achieve similar results.*

21

The Litigator

The Essential Role of the Litigator

Litigators manage disputes through every phase of the courtroom process—from pre-suit investigations and pleadings to discovery, trial, and appeal. Their work demands analytical precision, persuasive writing, and the ability to distill vast evidentiary records into clear, compelling legal narratives.

Common Challenges Faced by Litigators

The primary challenge is discovery "information overload," where critical facts can be buried within massive document productions and transcript records. Litigators must also guard against strategic blind spots—overlooking weaknesses in their own case—while managing the intensive drafting demands of motions, timelines, and trial preparation.

How AI Simplifies Litigation Tasks

AI operates as a tireless litigation assistant. Large language models can summarize transcripts, compare witness statements for inconsistencies, simulate opposing arguments for trial preparation, and generate first-draft pleadings, allowing counsel to devote more time to strategic analysis and courtroom advocacy.

Crafting Effective Prompts for Litigation Tasks

This section provides practical, role-specific prompts that enable litigators to employ large language models such as ChatGPT, Gemini, and CoCounsel as litigation support tools. The examples demonstrate how AI can assist with deposition preparation, discovery review, strategic risk analysis, motion drafting, and narrative development, turning the model into a dynamic legal sparring partner.

1. Deposition Preparation (Simulating Hostile Witnesses)

Scenario

A litigator is preparing to depose a hostile witness—a former Chief Financial Officer accused of inflating revenue figures. The attorney needs to practice questioning techniques against a witness who is evasive, defensive, and skilled at avoiding direct answers without making false statements.

> ***Prompt***
> *"Act as a hostile witness in a corporate fraud deposition. You are a former CFO accused of inflating revenue figures. I will ask you questions regarding the third-quarter financial statements. Respond with evasive, defensive answers typical of a witness attempting to avoid liability without making false statements. After each response, provide brief 'Meta-Commentary' in brackets explaining the weakness in my question that allowed you to evade it."*

How It Works

Using ChatGPT or Gemini, first enter the prompt. Next, begin the simulation by typing your first deposition question. Then submit. The AI will respond in character as the evasive witness and provide commentary on how your questioning can be improved. Continue this exchange to refine your questioning technique before conducting the real deposition.

2. Discovery Discrepancy Analysis

Scenario

A lawyer has received two conflicting witness statements regarding a motor vehicle accident. To prepare a trial timeline, the attorney must identify where the statements diverge as to the sequence of events, personal descriptions, and environmental conditions.

Prompt

"You are a senior litigation analyst. Based on the two witness statements provided below, create a comparative table identifying factual inconsistencies. Focus on: (1) the timeline of events, (2) the description of the driver, and (3) the weather conditions at the time of the incident."

How It Works

Using ChatGPT, Gemini, or CoCounsel, first enter the prompt. Next, paste or upload Witness Statement A and Witness Statement B into the chat interface. Then submit. The AI cross-references both accounts and generates a side-by-side comparison table highlighting contradictions and alignment points.

.

3. Case Strategy SWOT Analysis

Scenario

A partner seeks an objective early assessment of a breach-of-contract case in order to determine whether settlement discussions should begin or litigation should proceed. They want to identify potential weaknesses that might be obscured by confirmation bias.

> ***Prompt***
>
> *"Act as a neutral judicial clerk. Review the Case Fact Summary provided below. Perform a SWOT Analysis (Strengths, Weaknesses, Opportunities, and Threats) regarding the plaintiff's likelihood of success under [Insert Jurisdiction] contract law. Be highly critical and identify potential defenses the opposing party could raise."*

How It Works

Using ChatGPT or Perplexity, first enter the prompt with the relevant jurisdiction. Next, paste the anonymized Case Fact Summary from your notes. Then submit. The AI produces a detached, objective risk assessment that functions as a second-opinion strategy check.

4. Drafting a Motion in Limine (Excluding Evidence)

Scenario

Defense counsel must file a pre-trial motion to exclude a prejudicial email chain that is irrelevant to the core breach-of-contract claim. The argument must rely on Rule 403 of the Federal Rules of Evidence (or an equivalent local rule).

> ***Prompt***
>
> *"Act as a Defense Litigator. Draft the 'Argument' section of a Motion in Limine seeking to exclude an email chain dated [Insert Date] between the defendant and a third party. Argue that the evidence is irrelevant to the breach-of-contract claims and that any probative value is substantially outweighed by the risk of unfair prejudice under Federal Rule of Evidence 403 (or applicable jurisdiction). Cite general legal principles addressing character evidence and hearsay."*

How It Works

Using Gemini or ChatGPT, first enter the prompt. Next, paste the anonymized email content to provide context. Then submit. The AI generates a structured argument referencing relevant evidentiary rules, which can be refined with jurisdiction-specific case citations.

5. Opening Statement Narrative Builder

Scenario

A trial lawyer has assembled all factual evidence but struggles to convert timelines and bullet points into a persuasive jury narrative. They need a story-focused Opening Statement theme.

> ***Prompt***
>
> *"Act as a master storyteller and trial advocate. Review the Case Chronology provided below. Transform these facts into a compelling narrative for an Opening Statement in a medical malpractice trial. The theme of the case is 'A Failure to Listen.' Emphasize the human impact on the plaintiff, avoid legal jargon, and maintain a solemn but persuasive tone."*

How It Works

Using ChatGPT or Gemini, first enter the prompt. Next, paste your case chronology or bullet-point timeline below it. Then submit. The AI reshapes factual entries into a cohesive trial narrative with a clear thematic hook and emotional continuity.

22

Corporate Law

The Essential Role of the Corporate Lawyer

Corporate attorneys serve as the architects of business transactions. They structure deals, negotiate mergers, draft governing documents, and ensure that commercial agreements align with organizational strategy. Their work demands precision in risk allocation, clarity of contractual language, and the foresight to draft agreements that withstand ambiguity and future disputes.

Common Challenges Faced by Corporate Lawyers

Corporate practice involves several recurring pressures. "Drafting fatigue" arises from producing and revising repetitive boilerplate clauses across numerous agreements. Due diligence can require reviewing hundreds or thousands of contracts within tight timelines. Attorneys must also identify subtle risks in complex, cross-border arrangements—oversights that may escalate into significant post-closing disputes.

How AI Simplifies Corporate Tasks

AI's strength lies in pattern recognition, rapid text analysis, and sophisticated language generation. It can automate the drafting of standard clauses, examine large batches of contracts to extract key provisions during mergers and acquisitions due diligence, and propose redlines that reflect market norms and client interests. When used appropriately, AI significantly reduces time spent on routine tasks and enhances the accuracy of transactional work.

Crafting Effective Prompts for Corporate Tasks

This section provides tailored prompts for corporate practitioners engaged in transactions and governance. These examples illustrate how large language models can accelerate contract review, support the drafting of precise provisions, and simulate negotiation dynamics to strengthen client outcomes.

1. M&A Due Diligence (Risk Extraction)

Scenario

An associate is conducting due diligence for a merger and needs to review a batch of 50 supplier contracts. The goal is to identify if any contracts contain "Change of Control" provisions that would require the supplier's consent before the merger can proceed.

> ***Prompt***
>
> *"You are an M&A Due Diligence specialist. Based on the attached supplier contracts, extract every 'Change of Control' or 'Assignment' clause. Create a summary table listing: (1) Contract Name, (2) The specific Clause Language, and (3) A Risk Level assessment (Low/Medium/High) regarding whether third-party consent is required for the merger."*

How It Works

Using a tool like ChatGPT or Gemini, first, enter the prompt. Next, upload the batch of PDF or Word contracts. Then, submit. The AI will parse the documents and generate a structured risk register. This allows you to quickly identify which contracts require immediate attention for consent waivers, saving hours of manual reading.

2. Drafting a Shareholder Agreement Clause

Scenario

A lawyer needs to draft a precise "Right of First Refusal" (ROFR) clause for a startup with three co-founders. The clause must ensure that if one founder wants to sell their shares, the others have the right to buy them first.

> ***Prompt***
>
> *"Act as a senior corporate attorney. Draft a 'Right of First Refusal' (ROFR) clause for a Shareholder Agreement governed by [Insert Jurisdiction]. The clause must apply to any voluntary transfer of shares by a Founder. Include provisions for a 30-day notice period and clear valuation mechanics. The tone should be formal and protective of the non-selling shareholders."*

How It Works

Using ChatGPT or Microsoft Copilot, first, enter the prompt specifying the jurisdiction and constraints. Then, submit. The AI will generate a sophisticated draft clause. You can then copy this text into your master agreement and make minor refinements to fit the specific definitions of your document.

3. Negotiation "War Gaming"

Scenario

Counsel for a software buyer has drafted a strict indemnity clause in a SaaS agreement. They want to anticipate how the Seller's lawyer will push back so they can prepare counter-arguments or a compromise position.

> ***Prompt***
>
> *"I am representing the Buyer in a SaaS procurement deal. I have drafted the strict 'Unlimited Indemnity' clause provided below. Act as the Seller's General Counsel. Review the clause, explain why you would reject it based on market standards, and provide a 'redline' counter-proposal that limits the Seller's liability."*

How It Works

Using ChatGPT or Gemini, first, enter the prompt. Next, paste your draft indemnity clause directly below it. Then, submit. The AI will simulate the counter-party's logic and provide a marked-up version of the clause, giving you a preview of the negotiation battleground.

4. Board Meeting Minutes Summarization

Scenario

A junior associate has pages of unstructured notes from a three-hour Board of Directors meeting and must convert them into formal minutes that accurately reflect discussions, resolutions, and action items.

> ***Prompt***
>
> *"You are a Corporate Secretary. Review the rough meeting notes provided below. Convert them into formal Board Meeting Minutes. The output must include: (1) Date and Attendees, (2) Agenda Items discussed, (3) Exact wording of Resolutions passed, and (4) Action Items assigned. Remove all colloquialisms and off-topic discussion. Use a formal, passive voice."*

How It Works

Using ChatGPT or Gemini, first enter the prompt. Next, paste your meeting notes below it. Then submit. The AI reformats the material into compliant, professionally structured Board Minutes.

5. Term Sheet Generation (Letter of Intent)

Scenario

A partner receives key deal points over the phone from a client seeking to acquire a small manufacturing business. They need to quickly produce a non-binding Letter of Intent (LOI) to initiate the transaction.

> ***Prompt***
>
> *"Act as a Senior Transactional Attorney. Draft a non-binding Letter of Intent (LOI) for the acquisition of a manufacturing company based on the deal points listed below. Include standard sections for: Purchase Price ($5M), Earn-out ($1M over 2 years), Exclusivity Period (60 days), and Confidentiality. Clearly state that the letter is non-binding except for the confidentiality and exclusivity provisions."*

How It Works

Using ChatGPT or Gemini, first, enter the prompt. Next, paste your deal points below it. Then, submit. The AI generates a structured, professionally formatted Letter of Intent suitable for immediate client review.

23

Intellectual Property (IP) Law

The Essential Role of the IP Attorney

IP attorneys safeguard the core assets of innovation—ideas, brands, inventions, and creative expressions. Their work requires navigating complex global registries, drafting precise and technically accurate filings, and enforcing rights against infringers. Success in this field demands meticulous language, flawless classification, and extensive search capabilities to ensure that clients' intangible assets are fully protected.

Common Challenges Faced by IP Attorneys

The enormous volume of existing trademarks and patents makes Prior Art searches both time-consuming and vulnerable to oversight. Attorneys must also frequently translate dense technical claims into language that judges, juries, and non-technical clients can understand—an enduring challenge often referred to as the "translation problem."

How AI Simplifies IP Tasks

AI excels at search, pattern recognition, and technical simplification. It can rapidly analyze patent claims, compare trademark classes to estimate the likelihood of confusion, and produce draft Cease & Desist letters or IP agreements. Its ability to synthesize complex information helps IP practitioners move faster while reducing the risk of missed details.

Crafting Effective Prompts for IP Tasks

This section provides strategic prompts tailored for Intellectual Property professionals. Focused on technical precision and clear communication, these prompts demonstrate how to use AI to evaluate trademark conflicts, simplify patent claims, and generate essential IP enforcement documents.

1. Trademark "Likelihood of Confusion" Analysis

Scenario

A lawyer needs to determine whether a client's proposed brand name "EvokeTech" (software) may conflict with an existing registered mark "EvokeSystems" (IT services). They want a preliminary assessment using the DuPont Factors before ordering a full search report.

> ***Prompt***
>
> *"Act as a Trademark Attorney. Compare the proposed mark 'EvokeTech' (Class 9: Software) with the existing mark 'EvokeSystems' (Class 42: IT Services). Analyze the 'Likelihood of Confusion' using the standard DuPont Factors, focusing specifically on the similarity of the marks and the relatedness of the goods/services. Provide a risk assessment summary."*

How It Works

Using Perplexity AI or ChatGPT, first enter the prompt with the class details. Next, submit. The AI will perform a comparative analysis based on trademark principles, highlighting the factors that pose the greatest risk.

2. Patent Claim Simplification

Scenario

A litigator is preparing for a trial involving a complex engineering patent. They need to explain a dense technical claim to a jury of non-experts without losing the core legal meaning.

> ***Prompt***
>
> *"You are an expert in technical communication. Rewrite the following Patent Claim (Claim 1 from US Patent X) into plain English analogies suitable for a non-technical jury. Retain the core technical limitations but remove the 'patentese' jargon. Explain the function of the invention using a simple, real-world metaphor."*

How It Works

Using Gemini or ChatGPT, first enter the prompt. Next, paste the text of the complex patent claim. Then submit. The AI will translate the technical language into accessible explanations and provide metaphors suitable for courtroom communication.

3. Drafting a Cease & Desist Letter

Scenario

An IP attorney discovers a competitor using a logo that closely resembles their client's registered trademark and needs a formal Cease & Desist letter that is firm but leaves room for an amicable resolution.

> ***Prompt***
>
> *"Draft a formal Cease & Desist letter regarding Trademark Infringement. The recipient is using the mark [Infringing Mark] which infringes on my client's registered mark [Client Mark], Reg. No. [Number]. The tone should be firm but professional. Demand the immediate removal of the mark from their website and social media. Include a paragraph suggesting we are open to discussing a phase-out period to resolve this amicably."*

How It Works

Using ChatGPT or CoCounsel, first enter the prompt specifying the infringing marks. Then submit. The AI provides a refined letter that includes required legal warnings while maintaining a professional tone that supports potential settlement discussions.

4. IP Assignment Agreement (Work-for-Hire)

Scenario

A startup hires a freelance developer to build an app but fails to secure an agreement beforehand. The attorney must prepare an IP Assignment Agreement ensuring the company owns all resulting code and materials.

> ***Prompt***
>
> *"Draft an Intellectual Property Assignment Agreement for a software developer contractor. The agreement must explicitly state that all code, designs, and documentation created during the engagement are 'Works Made for Hire' and are the sole property of the Company. Include a 'Further Assurances' clause and a waiver of moral rights."*

How It Works

Using ChatGPT or Microsoft Copilot, first enter the prompt. Then submit. The AI produces a detailed agreement addressing copyright transfer, ownership, and post-engagement obligations.

5. Patent Office Action Response Summary

Scenario

A patent attorney receives a lengthy Office Action from the U.S. Patent and Trademark Office and needs a clear summary explaining which claims were rejected and why.

> ***Prompt***
>
> *"Act as a Patent Attorney. Analyze the attached text from the USPTO Office Action. Summarize the Examiner's grounds for rejection. Specifically, identify which Claims were rejected under Section 102 (Anticipation) and which under Section 103 (Obviousness), and briefly explain the Examiner's logic for each. Keep the language accessible for a client update email."*

How It Works

Using Gemini or ChatGPT , first enter the prompt. Next, upload the OCR text of the Office Action. Then submit. The AI breaks down the Examiner's reasoning into a concise summary suitable for a client update.

24

Employment & Labor Law

The Essential Role of the Employment Lawyer

Employment lawyers manage the human dimension of organizational governance. They oversee the employer–employee relationship by drafting employment contracts, designing workplace policies, mediating disputes, addressing discrimination and harassment claims, and guiding employers through sensitive termination decisions. Their work requires both legal precision and emotional intelligence.

Common Challenges Faced by Employment Lawyers

Employment law evolves rapidly, with continuous updates affecting remote work regulations, gig-economy classifications, wage-and-hour rules, and workplace accommodations. Lawyers must translate these regulatory shifts into clear, enforceable policies. They also face the challenge of crafting communications—such as termination notices or performance warnings—that are legally compliant, emotionally sensitive, and defensible in any legal forum.

How AI Simplifies Employment Tasks

AI can quickly audit handbooks for regulatory compliance, draft sensitive termination scripts, generate jurisdiction-specific policies, and assist in creating consistent documentation for performance management. Its ability to balance legal precision with empathetic language makes it particularly useful in workplace matters, where tone is often as critical as accuracy.

Crafting Effective Prompts for Employment Tasks

This section offers practical prompts designed for Employment and Labor law practitioners. These examples demonstrate how AI can support legal compliance, reduce documentation errors, and assist in preparing humane and clear workplace communications.

1. Remote Work Policy Generation

Scenario

An HR department requests outside counsel to draft a "Hybrid Work Policy" for a UK-based financial firm. The policy must balance employee flexibility with strict data-security requirements and clearly define eligibility to avoid discrimination risks.

> ***Prompt***
>
> *"Act as an Employment Law Specialist. Draft a 'Hybrid Remote Work Policy' for a UK-based financial firm. The policy must cover: (1) Eligibility criteria for hybrid work, (2) Mandatory data security requirements for home offices, (3) Core office hours for collaboration, and (4) The company's right to revoke remote status for performance issues. The tone should be professional and clear."*

How It Works

Using ChatGPT or Microsoft Copilot, first enter the prompt specifying the jurisdictional focus (UK) and key policy pillars. Then submit. The AI generates a structured policy document that can be refined to match the client's internal culture.

2. Sensitive Termination Script

Scenario

A company must lay off a long-term employee due to restructuring. Counsel needs to prepare a script that is legally accurate, compassionate, and consistent across managers to reduce litigation and emotional escalation.

> ***Prompt***
>
> *"Draft a script for a termination meeting due to 'Role Redundancy.' The employee has been with the company for 10 years. The script must be legally precise regarding the reason (restructuring) but empathetic in tone. Include talking points on severance packages, outplacement support, and the logistics of returning company property."*

How It Works

Using ChatGPT, first enter the prompt. Then submit. The AI provides a compassionate yet legally compliant script that HR can use to deliver consistent messaging during the meeting.

3. Performance Improvement Plan (PIP)

Scenario

A manager wants to terminate an employee for poor performance but lacks documentation. Counsel needs to prepare a Performance Improvement Plan that creates a defensible record and gives the employee a meaningful opportunity to improve.

> ***Prompt***
>
> *"Draft a 60-day Performance Improvement Plan (PIP) for a Sales Associate who is missing targets. The tone must be constructive but formal. Include sections for: (1) Specific Performance Deficiencies (e.g., missing quota by 20%), (2) Measurable Goals for the next 60 days, (3) Support resources provided by the company, and (4) The consequences of failing to meet these goals (up to termination)."*

How It Works

Using ChatGPT, first enter the prompt. Then submit. The AI produces a structured, objective plan focused on measurable performance rather than personality, supporting legal defensibility.

4. Settlement Agreement (Exit & Waiver)

Scenario

An employer and employee agree to a separation with severance. The lawyer must draft a Settlement and Release Agreement to ensure the departing employee waives all claims while complying with relevant legal requirements.

> ***Prompt***
>
> *"Act as a Senior Employment Lawyer. Draft a Settlement and Release Agreement for a departing employee. Key terms: The Company will pay 3 months of severance salary. In exchange, the Employee agrees to a full waiver and release of all claims (including age discrimination and wrongful dismissal). Include standard clauses for Confidentiality, Non-Disparagement, and Return of Company Property."*

How It Works

Using ChatGPT or Gemini, first enter the prompt. Then submit. The AI generates a comprehensive agreement that can then be adjusted to meet jurisdiction-specific waiver requirements.

5. Diversity, Equity, and Inclusion (DEI) Policy

Scenario

A mid-sized company is updating its handbook and needs a modern DEI statement that promotes inclusion while avoiding language that could unintentionally create reverse-discrimination exposure.

> **Prompt**
>
> "Draft a Diversity, Equity, and Inclusion (DEI) Policy statement for an Employee Handbook. The policy should articulate the company's commitment to a diverse workplace, outline the grievance process for discrimination complaints, and define 'inclusive behavior.' The tone should be welcoming and corporate, avoiding political language."

How It Works

Using ChatGPT, Microsoft Copilot, or Gemini, first enter the prompt. Then submit. The AI produces a polished, modern DEI policy suitable for immediate insertion into the company handbook.

25

The Legal Compliance & Operations

The Essential Role of Compliance Officers

Compliance professionals ensure organizational adherence to external regulations such as the General Data Protection Regulation (GDPR) and Foreign Corrupt Practices Act (FCPA) , as well as internal governance policies. Legal Operations (Legal Ops) teams drive efficiency by managing legal spend, workflow optimization, vendor oversight, and technology implementation across the legal function.

Common Challenges Faced by Compliance and Legal Operations

A key challenge is the persistent "compliance gap"—the disconnect between written policy and daily operational behavior. Continuous regulatory change makes manual policy review impractical, while Legal Ops teams struggle with fragmented billing data and inconsistent reporting from outside counsel.

How AI Simplifies Compliance Tasks

AI serves as a continuous monitoring assistant—auditing policies for regulatory gaps, normalizing billing data for invoicing accuracy, extracting actionable risks from regulations, and converting complex statutory requirements into practical compliance checklists.

Crafting Effective Prompts for Compliance Tasks

This section provides targeted prompts for Compliance Officers and Legal Operations teams. Focused on policy auditing, regulatory summarization, risk screening, and data standardization, these examples demonstrate how AI can function as an automated auditor and operational assistant to enhance efficiency while reducing regulatory exposure.

1. GDPR/Privacy Policy Audit

Scenario

A Data Privacy Officer needs to review the company's existing Privacy Policy, which has not been updated in three years. They must identify gaps against current General Data Protection Regulation requirements for international data transfers.

> ***Prompt***
>
> *"Act as a Data Privacy Officer. Review the attached Privacy Policy. Cross-reference it against the latest GDPR requirements, specifically focusing on international data transfers. Identify clauses that are outdated or missing. Output the findings as a 'Red Flag Report' with recommended remediations."*

How It Works

Using Perplexity or Gemini, first enter the prompt. Next, upload the existing Privacy Policy document in pdf or docx format. Then submit. The AI analyzes the text against current privacy law requirements and produces a gap report with suggested updates.

2. Invoice Narrative Cleanup (Legal Ops)

Scenario

A law firm is preparing a client invoice. Time-entry narratives contain abbreviations, shorthand, and typographical errors that must be standardized.

> **Prompt**
>
> *"You are a Legal Billing Coordinator. Review the list of time entry descriptions below. Rewrite them into clear, professional, full-sentence narratives suitable for a client invoice. Expand all abbreviations (for example, change 'tc' to 'Telephone conference with opposing counsel'). Do not alter dates or billing time amounts."*

How It Works

Using ChatGPT or Gemini, first enter the prompt. Next, paste the unedited billing narratives below it. Then submit. The AI converts shorthand descriptions into polished entries suitable for invoicing.

3. Vendor Risk Assessment Questionnaire

Scenario

A company is onboarding a cloud software provider. The Compliance Officer must conduct a security and data protection assessment before contract execution.

> ***Prompt***
>
> *"Create a 'Vendor Security and Compliance Questionnaire' for a new Software as a Service provider. Generate 10 targeted questions covering: (1) data encryption standards, (2) server locations and data sovereignty, (3) incident response procedures, and (4) compliance with International Organization for Standardization 27001 or SOC 2 certification requirements."*

How It Works

Using ChatGPT, first enter the prompt. Then submit. The AI produces a detailed screening questionnaire ready for direct distribution to the vendor.

4. Regulatory Change Executive Summary

Scenario

A new Anti-Money Laundering (AML) law has been enacted. The General Counsel needs a concise one-page executive briefing outlining its implications for business leadership.

> ***Prompt***
>
> *"Act as General Counsel advising the Chief Executive Officer. Summarize the business impact of the [Insert Name of New Act or Law]. Focus on: (1) new reporting obligations, (2) penalty increases for non-compliance, and (3) required compliance budget adjustments. Limit the briefing to one page and use bullet points for clarity."*

How It Works

Using Perplexity or Gemini, first enter the prompt. Next, provide the text or link to the new regulation. Then submit. The AI distills the statute into a concise executive briefing tailored to business leaders.

5. Compliance Training Scenario Generator

Scenario

The Legal Operations team is developing a mandatory training module on Anti-Bribery and Foreign Corrupt Practices Act compliance. Realistic scenarios are needed to test employee judgment.

> ***Prompt***
>
> *"Create three realistic hypothetical compliance scenarios for Anti-Bribery and Foreign Corrupt Practices Act training:*
>
> *Scenario 1: Offering a gift to a government official.*
>
> *Scenario 2: Paying a 'consulting fee' to a third-party intermediary.*
>
> *Scenario 3: Sponsoring an extravagant client entertainment event.*
>
> *For each scenario, create a multiple-choice question with four options and identify the correct answer with a brief legal explanation."*

How It Works

Using ChatGPT or Gemini, first enter the prompt. Then submit. The AI generates training-ready scenarios complete with questions and compliance explanations, allowing legal teams to deploy interactive training without manual content development.

26

Real Estate & Property Law

The Essential Role of the Real Estate Lawyer

Real estate attorneys oversee the legal transfer and use of property across residential and commercial transactions, including closings, leasing, zoning disputes, title reviews, and conveyancing. Their work demands exceptional precision, as even minor errors in legal descriptions, lien searches, or recording documents can create title defects lasting decades.

Common Challenges Faced by Real Estate Lawyers

This practice often involves intensive document review—such as dissecting multi-dozen-page commercial leases—while operating under rigid transactional deadlines. Lawyers must manage extensive documentation trails of deeds, riders, disclosures, and financing instruments, alongside continuously changing zoning codes and local regulatory standards.

How AI Simplifies Real Estate Tasks

Artificial intelligence functions as a lease-review assistant and compliance organizer. It can extract core financial obligations from lengthy lease agreements, generate tailored closing checklists based on transaction details, and draft standardized contract riders, thereby reducing time spent on manual review and repetitive drafting.

Crafting Effective Prompts for Real Estate Tasks

This section provides practical prompts for real estate professionals. The examples demonstrate how artificial intelligence can be used to summarize commercial leases, draft legally compliant eviction notices, interpret zoning regulations, and create accurate closing checklists—all while improving transactional efficiency and minimizing error risk.

1. Commercial Lease Abstraction

Scenario

A lawyer must review a sixty-page commercial lease and prepare a concise, one-page abstract summarizing the most critical financial and operational terms for a client executive.

> ***Prompt***
>
> *"Act as a Real Estate Attorney. Review the attached Commercial Lease Agreement and prepare a 'Lease Abstract' summarizing the following key terms: (1) Base Rent and Rent Escalation provisions, (2) Security Deposit requirements, (3) Lease Commencement and Expiration Dates, (4) Renewal Options, and (5) Tenant Maintenance obligations, including Common Area Maintenance charges. Present the findings in a structured table."*

How It Works

Using ChatGPT or Gemini, first enter the prompt. Next, upload the lease document in PDF or text format. Then submit. The AI extracts the relevant contractual data and organizes it into a clean summary table, saving extensive review time while preserving accuracy.

2. Drafting a Residential Repair Rider

Scenario

A buyer wishes to ensure that a roof repair is completed before closing. The attorney must draft a repair rider to supplement the standard residential purchase contract.

> ***Prompt***
>
> *"Draft a 'Repair Rider' for a residential real estate contract of sale stating that the Seller agrees to repair the roof leak in the master bedroom prior to closing. Require the work to be completed by a licensed contractor and mandate that receipts and warranties be delivered to the Buyer during the final walk-through. Include a provision allowing the Buyer to delay closing or escrow funds if repairs are incomplete."*

How It Works

Using ChatGPT, Gemini, or Microsoft Copilot, first enter the prompt. Then submit. The AI generates a professionally structured rider clause ready for integration into the purchase contract template.

3. Eviction Notice Generation

Scenario

A landlord seeks to initiate eviction proceedings against a commercial tenant for nonpayment of June rent totaling $5,000. The attorney must draft a jurisdiction-specific Notice to Cure compliant with statutory service requirements.

> ***Prompt***
>
> *"Draft a formal '3-Day Notice to Pay Rent or Quit' for a commercial tenancy in [Insert City/County]. The tenant owes $5,000 in past-due rent for the month of July. The notice must cite the applicable local property-code statutes governing service of notice and the tenant's right to cure. The tone should be strictly formal and legally precise."*

How It Works

Using ChatGPT, first enter the prompt and specify the applicable jurisdiction. Then submit. The AI generates the notice template with statutory references. Final verification against current local law should always be conducted before service.

4. Zoning Regulation Summary

Scenario

A real estate developer intends to build a multi-family structure on property currently zoned for single-family use. The attorney must summarize the criteria and procedural steps required for obtaining a zoning variance.

> ***Prompt***
>
> *"Act as a Land Use Attorney. Summarize the requirements for obtaining a 'Zoning Variance' for residential density in [Insert City/County]. Explain the legal 'hardship' standards reviewed by the Zoning Board of Appeals and list each procedural step required to file and prosecute a variance application."*

How It Works

Using Perplexity AI or Gemini, first enter the prompt with the precise municipality specified. Then submit. The AI retrieves municipal zoning codes and condenses the legal standards and application process into a concise advisory summary.

5. Closing Checklist Generator

Scenario

A complex hotel acquisition requires a comprehensive document checklist to ensure all closing materials and regulatory transfers are completed accurately.

> ***Prompt***
>
> *"Create a comprehensive 'Closing Checklist' for the acquisition of a commercial hotel property. Organize the checklist into the following categories: (1) Real Estate Documents (deeds, title insurance, environmental reports), (2) Corporate Authority Documents, (3) Financing and Loan Documents, and (4) Operational Transfers (liquor licenses, permits, service contracts). Format as a checkbox-style task list."*

How It Works

Using ChatGPT, first enter the prompt. Then submit. The AI generates a comprehensive closing checklist that helps structure transactional workflows and delegate responsibilities among the closing team.

27

Family & Matrimonial Law

The Essential Role of the Family Lawyer

Family lawyers handle the most personal and emotionally sensitive legal issues, including divorce, child custody, spousal support, and prenuptial agreements. Their practice combines rigorous legal advocacy—such as asset classification and property division—with interpersonal skills focused on empathy, conflict management, and client guidance during emotionally volatile proceedings.

Common Challenges Faced by Family Lawyers

Key challenges include managing highly emotional clients, organizing disordered financial disclosures involving bank records and debts, and drafting parenting plans detailed enough to anticipate scheduling disputes, holidays, and communication protocols in order to minimize future conflict.

How AI Simplifies Family Law Tasks

Artificial intelligence functions as a neutral drafting and organizational assistant. It can convert scattered financial data into asset-division tables, produce balanced parenting schedules, and reframe emotionally charged written communications into professional, court-appropriate correspondence.

Crafting Effective Prompts for Family Law Tasks

This section presents prompts specifically designed for the sensitive practice of Family Law. The examples demonstrate how artificial intelligence can assist attorneys in drafting comprehensive parenting plans, organizing complex financial disclosures for equitable distribution, and facilitating client communications that reduce conflict and preserve courtroom credibility.

1. Parenting Plan Drafting

Scenario

A lawyer must prepare a custody schedule for parents who live thirty minutes apart and remain within the same school district. The goal is to implement a 2-2-3 parenting rotation with clearly defined exchanges and holiday arrangements to avoid ambiguity and enforcement disputes.

> ***Prompt***
>
> *"Draft a 'Parenting Time Schedule' using a 2-2-3 rotation for two parents residing in the same school district. Define explicitly: (1) pick-up and drop-off times and locations (school versus residence), (2) alternating holiday schedules for Thanksgiving and Christmas, and (3) required communication protocols between parents (email only). The tone should be neutral, child-focused, and court-appropriate."*

How It Works

Using ChatGPT or Microsoft Copilot, first enter the prompt. Then submit. The AI produces a detailed custody framework incorporating rotation schedules, holiday divisions, and communication standards, which you can customize further to reflect client-specific preferences or court requirements.

2. Asset Division Spreadsheet (Equitable Distribution)

Scenario

A client submits an unorganized list of marital assets and debts—such as a home, retirement accounts, vehicles, and outstanding loans. The lawyer must visualize an equitable fifty-fifty distribution to support settlement negotiations.

> ***Prompt***
>
> *"Act as a Divorce Financial Planner. Review the list of marital assets and debts provided below. Create a 'Net Worth Settlement Statement' table showing item values, allocations to each spouse, and any equalization payments needed to achieve a 50/50 division of the total net marital estate."*

How It Works

Using ChatGPT or Gemini, first enter the prompt. Next, paste the asset and debt list with values. Then submit. The AI organizes the financial data into a clear table and calculates the necessary adjustments to reach an equitable division outcome.

3. De-Escalation of Client Communications

Scenario

A client drafts a hostile email to their former spouse regarding missed visitation. The attorney must neutralize the tone to protect the client's credibility and prevent negative courtroom impressions.

> ***Prompt***
>
> *"Review the following email draft written by my client to their former spouse. Rewrite it using the BIFF method—Brief, Informative, Friendly, and Firm. Remove all emotional or accusatory language. Restrict the message to factual statements about the missed visitation and a polite request to reschedule. Ensure the final version would be appropriate for family-court review."*

How It Works

Using ChatGPT, first enter the prompt. Next, paste the client's original draft below it and submit. The AI strips emotional content, restructures the language, and produces a professional email that preserves legal standing while advancing resolution.

4. Prenuptial Agreement – Social Media Clause

Scenario

A client requests a clause in their prenuptial agreement restricting online posting of private family information to protect personal privacy and children's exposure.

> ***Prompt***
>
> *"Draft a 'Social Media and Privacy' clause for a Prenuptial Agreement. Prohibit both parties from posting photographs, videos, or private personal information concerning the other spouse or any minor children on social media platforms without prior written consent. Include an enforceable liquidated damages provision for breach."*

How It Works

Using ChatGPT, first enter the prompt. Then submit. The AI drafts a modern privacy clause designed to address digital-age concerns while maintaining contractual enforceability standards.

5. Client Explanation of Alimony

Scenario

A primary-earning spouse does not understand why spousal support may be required. The lawyer needs a compassionate, plain-language explanation that accurately reflects the purpose of rehabilitative alimony.

> ***Prompt***
>
> *"Explain 'Rehabilitative Alimony' to a client who is the primary income earner. Use non-legal language and simple analogies. Emphasize that support is intended to give the lower-earning spouse time to gain education or job skills to become financially independent—not as punishment. Limit the explanation to 200 words."*

How It Works

Using ChatGPT, first enter the prompt. Then submit. The AI generates a concise, empathetic explanation that aligns client understanding with legal standards and manages expectations effectively.

28

Criminal & Defense Law

The Essential Role of the Criminal Lawyer

Criminal lawyers—both defense counsel and prosecutors—operate where personal liberty is on the line. Their work includes analyzing police reports, navigating statutory sentencing guidelines, negotiating plea agreements, and presenting evidence and arguments before judges and juries.

Common Challenges Faced by Criminal Lawyers

Criminal practice demands the continuous review of extensive evidence, including body-camera footage, surveillance recordings, and lengthy police transcripts. Attorneys must identify subtle inconsistencies that can undermine witness credibility and translate technical forensic evidence into clear narratives that lay jurors can understand.

How AI Simplifies Criminal Law Tasks

Artificial intelligence functions as a legal investigative assistant. It can summarize law-enforcement narratives to flag contradictions, draft foundational motions—such as suppression requests based on constitutional violations—and generate targeted cross-examination questions designed to expose bias or unreliable testimony.

Crafting Effective Prompts for Criminal Law Tasks

This section presents AI prompts designed for criminal defense litigation. These examples demonstrate practical uses of artificial intelligence for preparing cross-examinations, detecting evidentiary weaknesses, developing mitigation narratives for sentencing, shaping jury selection strategies, and clarifying the legal standard of reasonable doubt.

1. Cross-Examination Preparation

Scenario

A defense attorney is preparing to cross-examine an arresting officer who claims the defendant appeared intoxicated during a traffic stop. The attorney seeks to challenge the subjectivity of the officer's observations and introduce alternative explanations for the defendant's performance during field sobriety testing.

> ***Prompt***
>
> *"Act as a Defense Attorney. Draft a sequence of leading cross-examination questions for a police officer regarding the administration of Field Sobriety Tests. Emphasize possible external factors—including uneven road surfaces, weather conditions, anxiety, and physical fatigue—that could account for poor performance and create reasonable doubt about intoxication."*

How It Works

Using ChatGPT, first enter the prompt. Then submit. The AI generates a structured series of "yes or no" questions designed to maintain witness control while highlighting variables that undermine the reliability of the officer's conclusions.

2. Sentencing Mitigation Memorandum

Scenario

A client has entered a guilty plea. Defense counsel must prepare a memorandum urging the court to impose probation rather than incarceration by presenting the client's background, rehabilitative efforts, and genuine remorse in mitigation of sentencing.

> ***Prompt***
>
> *"Draft the 'Personal History' section of a Sentencing Mitigation Memorandum. The defendant is a 25-year-old first-time offender. Highlight struggles with poverty, lack of mentorship, recent employment stability, community support, and sincere remorse. The tone should humanize the defendant while persuasively justifying a downward departure from sentencing guidelines."*

How It Works

Using ChatGPT or Gemini, first enter the prompt. Next, paste the bullet-point list of the client's factual background. Then submit. The AI synthesizes these details into a compelling narrative that presents the defendant as a rehabilitative candidate rather than a sentencing statistic.

3. Police Report Inconsistency Analysis

Scenario

The attorney possesses both the initial police incident report and the arresting officer's later deposition transcript. The attorney suspects factual discrepancies, particularly regarding when Miranda warnings were administered.

> ***Prompt***
>
> *"Compare the two text excerpts provided below: (1) the Police Incident Report and (2) the Officer's Deposition Transcript. Identify any factual inconsistencies relating to the timing of the arrest and the delivery of Miranda warnings."*

How It Works

Using CoCounsel or Gemini, first enter the prompt. Next, paste both document excerpts. Then submit. The AI performs a comparative analysis and flags conflicting statements that may support a Motion to Suppress or impeachment at trial.

4. Jury Selection (Voir Dire) Development

Scenario

The attorney is preparing jury selection for a drug-possession trial and must identify potential jurors who may harbor biases toward law enforcement or defendants dealing with substance-use issues.

Prompt

"Draft ten Voir Dire questions for a drug possession trial designed to identify juror bias concerning addiction, drug enforcement, and law-enforcement credibility. Include a mix of open-ended questions for discussion and targeted questions that may support 'for cause' challenges."

How It Works

Using ChatGPT or Gemini, first enter the prompt. Then submit. The AI generates a diversified set of questions that assist in evaluating jurors' predispositions and assembling a balanced, impartial jury panel.

5. Closing Argument – Explaining Reasonable Doubt

Scenario

The prosecution's case relies principally on circumstantial evidence. Defense counsel needs a memorable narrative device to explain the legal concept of reasonable doubt during closing arguments.

> ***Prompt***
>
> *"Draft a closing-argument segment explaining 'Reasonable Doubt' using a relatable non-legal analogy—such as an incomplete puzzle—to demonstrate that uncertainty or guesswork requires acquittal. Maintain a solemn, empowering, and juror-focused tone."*

How It Works

Using ChatGPT, first enter the prompt. Then submit. The AI crafts a rhetorical passage that converts the abstract legal standard into an accessible narrative, reinforcing the jury's obligation to acquit in the presence of doubt.

29

Immigration Law

The Essential Role of the Immigration Lawyer

Immigration lawyers guide individuals, families, and employers through complex border and status systems to secure visas, lawful permanent residence, asylum protections, and work authorization. Their practice is highly procedural, form-intensive, and sensitive to rapidly shifting regulatory and political landscapes.

Common Challenges Faced by Immigration Lawyers

Among the most significant challenges is the evidentiary burden—assembling hundreds of pages of documentation to prove family relationships, professional credentials, or persecution claims. Attorneys must also navigate inflexible government filing systems where minor technical errors can trigger costly delays or outright denials.

How AI Simplifies Immigration Tasks

Artificial intelligence supports immigration practice by organizing extensive evidence, drafting legally compliant affidavits, researching up-to-date country-conditions reports, and synthesizing professional achievements to support petitions based on "Extraordinary Ability" classifications such as the O-1 and EB-1 visa categories.

Crafting Effective Prompts for Immigration Tasks

This section presents prompts designed for immigration attorneys handling visa petitions, asylum claims, and client communications. These examples demonstrate how to use AI tools to draft persuasive regulatory arguments, conduct international human-rights research, and translate complex procedural requirements into clear guidance for clients.

1. O-1 Visa "Extraordinary Ability" Support Letter

Scenario

A lawyer is preparing an O-1 visa petition for a professional graphic designer. They must draft a formal support letter synthesizing awards, publications, and leadership roles to demonstrate that the beneficiary qualifies as an individual of "extraordinary ability."

> ***Prompt***
> *"Act as an Immigration Attorney. Draft a persuasive support letter for an O-1A visa petition. The beneficiary is a Graphic Designer. Structure the argument to demonstrate compliance with the criteria for: (1) Leading or critical roles for distinguished organizations, and (2) Receipt of major nationally recognized awards. Use the facts provided below to substantiate the claim of 'sustained national acclaim.'"*

How It Works

Using ChatGPT or Microsoft Copilot, first enter the prompt. Next, paste the client's curriculum vitae and supporting award documentation. Then submit. The AI composes a narrative letter aligning the beneficiary's evidence with the applicable United States Citizenship and Immigration Services regulatory criteria, producing a draft suitable for attorney review and refinement.

2. Asylum Affidavit Support

Scenario

A lawyer is representing a client from [Country X] seeking asylum based on political persecution. The attorney requires objective background evidence to reinforce the client's sworn affidavit.

> ***Prompt***
>
> *"Act as a Human Rights Researcher. Summarize current 'Country Conditions' in [Insert Country] concerning treatment of political dissidents and journalists. Focus on developments reported in 2023–2024. Cite incidents or findings from reputable sources, including the U.S. State Department and Amnesty International, that support a persecution claim."*

How It Works

Using Perplexity AI or Gemini, first, enter the prompt specifying the jurisdiction. Then submit. The AI retrieves relevant public human-rights reporting and summarizes key findings, producing corroborative material that can be referenced or appended to the asylum affidavit.

3. Client Explanation of Visa Processing Options

Scenario

A client does not understand the distinction between "Adjustment of Status" and "Consular Processing." The lawyer needs to send a brief explanatory email outlining both options.

> ***Prompt***
>
> *"Write an email explaining the difference between 'Adjustment of Status' (applying from within the United States) and 'Consular Processing' (applying at a U.S. consulate abroad). Use plain English. Identify the primary pros and cons of each option, focusing on estimated processing times and travel restrictions."*

How It Works

Using ChatGPT, first enter the prompt. Then submit. The AI produces a clear client-ready explanation that converts technical procedural distinctions into accessible guidance to support informed decision-making.

4. Request for Evidence (RFE) Response Strategy

Scenario

United States Citizenship and Immigration Services has issued a Request for Evidence questioning the bona fide nature of a marriage supporting a permanent-residence petition. The lawyer must determine what additional documentation may strengthen the record.

> ***Prompt***
>
> *"I received a Request for Evidence in a marriage-based Green Card case questioning the bona fides of the relationship. Generate a comprehensive checklist of secondary evidence demonstrating a shared life beyond joint financial accounts. Provide creative examples such as travel records, gym memberships, affidavits, photographs, and family correspondence."*

How It Works

Using ChatGPT or Gemini, first, enter the prompt as written. Then submit. The AI generates a structured checklist of supplemental evidence categories that can be requested from the client to satisfy evidentiary concerns raised by immigration authorities.

5. Translation and Simplification of Legal Notices

Scenario

A client with limited English proficiency receives a complex Notice of Action and becomes concerned about their case status. The lawyer must translate the legal notice into understandable, reassuring instructions.

> ***Prompt***
>
> *"Rewrite the following paragraph from a United States Citizenship and Immigration Services Notice of Action into simple, Grade-5-level English. Remove all legal jargon. Clearly explain:*
>
> *(1) What the notice says,*
>
> *(2) That the notice reflects a positive development (approval), and*
>
> *(3) What the client must do next."*

How It Works

Using ChatGPT, first enter the prompt. Next, paste the notice text. Then submit. The AI simplifies the content into plain-language guidance, allowing the attorney to quickly reassure and inform the client while preserving procedural accuracy.

30

Tax Law

The Essential Role of the Tax Lawyer

Tax lawyers advise individuals and businesses on navigating local, national, and international tax systems. Their work includes transaction structuring to minimize lawful tax exposure, dispute resolution with revenue authorities, and ongoing compliance planning.

Common Challenges Faced by Tax Lawyers

Tax law is characterized by statutory complexity, constant legislative change, and technical interpretation challenges. Attorneys must decipher ambiguous provisions and translate intricate tax obligations into actionable guidance for clients seeking clear financial answers.

How AI Simplifies Tax Law Workflows

AI tools support tax practice by researching complex tax statutes, summarizing legislative updates, and modeling alternative tax scenarios for clients. When used appropriately, these systems enhance research efficiency, analysis clarity, and client communication.

Crafting Effective Prompts for Tax Tasks

This section highlights the precision required in tax practice. The following prompts demonstrate how artificial intelligence tools may assist with statutory interpretation, client explanation, regulatory monitoring, advocacy drafting, and international tax planning.

1. Tax Code Research Memo

Scenario

A client plans to exchange commercial real estate and seeks guidance on the tax implications of a "Like-Kind Exchange" under Section 1031 of the United States Internal Revenue Code.

> *Prompt*
>
> *"Act as a tax attorney. Write a research memorandum summarizing the requirements for a Section 1031 Like-Kind Exchange under the United States Internal Revenue Code. Explain the statutory timelines for identifying and closing on replacement property and outline which property types qualify for exchange treatment."*

How It Works

Using an AI research platform such as Microsoft Copilot or Gemini, first enter the prompt. Then submit. The AI generates a structured statutory summary outlining key eligibility criteria and procedural rules, forming the foundation for professional advisory guidance.

2. Client Explanation: Home Office Deductions

Scenario

A freelance graphic designer seeks advice on whether home office expenses qualify as deductible business expenses.

> ***Prompt***
>
> *"Explain the Internal Revenue Service Home Office Deduction rules to a freelance graphic designer using plain language. Focus on the 'Exclusive Use' test, clarifying that occasional work at a dining-room table does not qualify. Provide practical examples of compliant and non-compliant usage."*

How It Works

Using an AI drafting tool such as ChatGPT, first enter the prompt and submit. The AI produces a clear, client-friendly explanation designed to translate complex statutory standards into understandable guidance.

3. Regulatory Update Summary

Scenario

New legislation modifies corporate tax rates and alters the treatment of research and development expenditures. Firm partners require a concise briefing.

> ***Prompt***
>
> *"Summarize the key corporate tax provisions of the [Insert Name of New Tax Act]. Focus on changes to the corporate tax rate and the treatment of research-and-development expenses. Present the information in a 'Before vs. After' comparison table."*

How It Works

Using an AI research platform such as Perplexity AI or Gemini, first enter the prompt specifying the legislation. Then submit. The AI scans legislative sources and produces a comparative table for rapid professional review.

4. Penalty Abatement Letter

Scenario

A client failed to meet a filing deadline due to hospitalization and received an assessed penalty. Legal counsel must request penalty relief based on reasonable cause.

> ***Prompt***
>
> *"Draft a formal letter to the Internal Revenue Service requesting penalty abatement for late filing based on 'Reasonable Cause.' Cite hospitalization due to a medical emergency during the filing period. Maintain a respectful and factual tone and reference the appropriate sections of the Internal Revenue Manual recognizing illness as reasonable cause."*

How It Works

Using an AI drafting platform such as ChatGPT, first enter the prompt and submit. The AI produces a professionally formatted advocacy letter referencing applicable administrative guidance to support penalty abatement.

5. International Tax Scenario: Residency Status

Scenario

A client is relocating from the United Kingdom to Dubai and seeks guidance on the basic requirements for ending United Kingdom tax residency.

> ***Prompt***
>
> *"Explain the United Kingdom 'Statutory Residence Test' (SRT). Summarize the 'Automatic Overseas Test' component and provide a checklist of criteria required for classification as a non-resident for the tax year."*

How It Works

Using an AI explanatory platform such as ChatGPT, first enter the prompt and submit. The AI breaks down the statutory test into a concise planning checklist suitable for preliminary residency determinations.

31

Media & Entertainment Law

The Essential Role of the Media Lawyer

Media lawyers represent artists, influencers, creators, and production companies in protecting creative works and commercial rights. Their practice focuses on intellectual property management, talent contracting, content review for defamation risk, and regulatory compliance in traditional and digital media environments.

Common Challenges Faced by Media Lawyers

The fast-paced nature of digital media creates ongoing legal complexity. Attorneys review non-standard influencer agreements, secure real-time music licensing clearances, and advise clients responding to social-media reputation risks and public-relations disputes.

How Artificial Intelligence Simplifies Media Law Tasks

In secure environments, artificial intelligence tools assist with contract review, rights analysis, and content risk screening. These systems can identify problematic intellectual-property transfer clauses, explain music licensing structures—such as synchronization and master-use rights—and analyze media content for potential defamation exposure.

Crafting Effective Prompts for Media Tasks

This section provides targeted prompts for the modern media and entertainment practice. Each example demonstrates how artificial intelligence can support influencer contract review, rights-enforcement correspondence, defamation screening, and content licensing analysis to ensure creators and production clients remain protected.

1. Influencer Agreement Review

Scenario

A lawyer represents a YouTube creator offered a sponsorship agreement. The contract must be reviewed to ensure it does not grant the brand ownership of the creator's full content library rather than a limited promotional license.

> ***Prompt***
>
> *"Act as an entertainment lawyer. Review the attached Brand Sponsorship Agreement clause addressing intellectual property rights. Determine whether the clause grants the brand perpetual ownership of the influencer's content or merely a limited-use license. If ownership is granted, draft a redline negotiation comment requesting replacement language establishing a limited usage license instead."*

How It Works

Using an AI contract-analysis platform such as ChatGPT or Gemini, first enter the prompt. Next, paste the relevant intellectual property clause into the system. Then submit. The AI evaluates the scope of rights transfer and generates recommended negotiation language protecting the creator's ownership interests.

2. Cease-and-Desist: Image Rights and Copyright

Scenario

A website is selling merchandise bearing a celebrity client's images without authorization. Legal counsel must draft a formal takedown notice asserting right-of-publicity and copyright claims.

> ***Prompt***
>
> *"Draft a cease-and-desist letter to an online retailer for violations of the Right of Publicity and copyright law. The retailer is selling merchandise displaying the name and images of [Insert Client Name] without authorization. Demand immediate removal of the offending items and an accounting of profits. Cite applicable [Insert jurisdiction] Civil Code provisions governing personality rights."*

How It Works

Using an AI drafting tool such as ChatGPT, first enter the prompt with the relevant client name and jurisdiction details. Then submit. The AI will generate a jurisdiction-specific enforcement letter tailored to right-of-publicity infringement claims.

3. Defamation Risk Analysis

Scenario

A journalist plans to publish an investigative article and seeks counsel to identify statements that could result in a libel claim.

> ***Prompt***
>
> *"Review the following article excerpt for potential defamation (libel) risk. Identify statements presented as factual assertions versus protected expressions of opinion. Highlight any passages alleging criminal conduct or professional incompetence that could raise liability concerns."*

How It Works

Using an AI review platform such as ChatGPT or Gemini, first enter the prompt. Next, paste the article text. Then submit. The AI will flag high-risk statements requiring additional verification or editorial revision prior to publication.

4. Music Licensing Clause: Synchronization Rights

Scenario

A filmmaker intends to use a popular song in an independent film and must understand why two separate licenses are required for lawful use.

> ***Prompt***
>
> *"Explain the difference between a synchronization license (for musical composition rights) and a master-use license (for sound recording rights). Clarify why both licenses are required to use a commercial song in a film. Draft a simplified contract clause securing synchronization rights from the music publisher."*

How It Works

Using an AI platform such as ChatGPT or CoCounsel, first enter the prompt, then submit. The AI will clarify the dual-rights structure governing music use and supply sample contract language demonstrating synchronization license acquisition.

5. Talent Agreement Negotiation Support

Scenario

A recording artist is negotiating a management contract and seeks legal guidance on the fairness of proposed compensation percentages, exclusivity terms, and termination clauses. The lawyer must conduct an initial clause analysis and prepare recommendations before entering negotiations.

> ***Prompt***
>
> *"Act as an entertainment attorney reviewing a music management agreement. Analyze the following clauses in the provided contract: (1) commission percentage, (2) contract term length and renewal provisions, (3) exclusivity obligations, and (4) termination and exit rights. Identify provisions that may disadvantage the artist, note any industry-standard benchmarks, and suggest alternative language to improve fairness."*

How It Works

Using an AI legal drafting platform such as CoCounsel or ChatGPT, first enter the prompt. Next, upload the relevant contract in pdf or docx format, then submit. The AI will evaluate each provision against common industry standards, highlights potentially unfavorable terms, and proposes balanced language options to support attorney-led negotiation and contract revision.

32

Health Law

The Essential Role of the Health Lawyer

Health lawyers advise healthcare providers, insurers, and life-science organizations on regulatory compliance under statutes such as the Health Insurance Portability and Accountability Act (HIPAA) and oversight by the Food and Drug Administration (FDA). Their work includes transactional support, malpractice risk management, bioethics guidance, and patient-consent governance, ensuring medical services operate within lawful and ethical boundaries.

Common Challenges Faced by Health Lawyers

Health law is characterized by dense regulation and strict privacy obligations. Attorneys must apply statutes such as the Physician Self-Referral Law (Stark Law) while converting complex clinical records into legally defensible analyses for litigation, auditing, and compliance reporting.

How Artificial Intelligence Simplifies Health Law Tasks

Within secure environments, artificial intelligence systems assist by redacting Personally Identifiable Information (PII), summarizing large medical records, and drafting plain-language patient consent documents. When used responsibly, these tools increase efficiency while supporting regulatory compliance and confidentiality protections.

Crafting Effective Prompts for Health Law Tasks

This section presents specialized prompts tailored to healthcare legal practice. With a focus on regulatory compliance and patient privacy, each example demonstrates how artificial intelligence tools can be used to assess HIPAA breach risks, generate plain-language consent forms, analyze medical litigation records, clarify regulatory constraints, and interpret statutory guidance for client advisory purposes.

1. HIPAA Breach Risk Assessment

Scenario

A hospital reports that a laptop containing unencrypted patient name lists and medical record numbers was stolen. Legal counsel must determine whether the incident qualifies as a "reportable breach" under HIPAA based on the probability that protected health information was compromised.

> ***Prompt***
> *"Act as a HIPAA compliance expert. Review the facts of a potential data incident: A laptop was stolen containing unencrypted names and medical record numbers; however, the device was password-protected (not encrypted). Analyze the Four-Factor Risk Assessment to determine the probability of compromise. Outline the arguments for and against classifying the incident as a reportable breach."*

How It Works

Using a research-capable AI platform, such as Perplexity AI or Gemini, first enter the prepared prompt. Then submit. The AI evaluates the facts against the HIPAA regulatory risk factors—including data sensitivity, unauthorized access, likelihood of acquisition, and mitigation measures—providing a reasoned foundation for professional advisory conclusions.

2. Patient Informed Consent Form

Scenario

A medical clinic is launching a new telehealth service. Legal counsel must draft a patient consent form explaining the risks of virtual consultations—including technical failures and privacy limitations—in language appropriate for a fifth-grade reading level.

> ***Prompt***
>
> *"Draft a 'Telehealth Informed Consent' form for a medical clinic using plain language at a Grade-5 reading level. Clearly explain: (1) what telehealth is, (2) the risk that technology may fail (such as video freezing or dropped connections), and (3) that the physician cannot conduct a physical examination during virtual visits. Include a patient signature block."*

How It Works

Using an AI drafting tool such as ChatGPT, first enter the prompt and then submit. The AI will generate a compliant consent form written in simplified language, prioritizing patient comprehension and reducing the risk of liability associated with inadequate disclosures or incomplete informed consent.

3. Medical Record Summarization (Litigation Support)

Scenario

Defense counsel in a malpractice case receives 500 pages of clinical documentation. A concise timeline of the patient's vital signs during the 24 hours following surgery is required to assess potential negligence.

Prompt

"Act as a legal nurse consultant. Review the anonymized text of the patient's medical chart. Create a chronological timeline of vital signs—including blood pressure, heart rate, and temperature—covering the first 24 hours after surgery. Flag all readings that fall outside standard clinical ranges."

How It Works

Using document-analysis platforms such as CoCounsel or Gemini, first enter the prompt. Next, upload the optical character recognition (OCR) text of the medical records after ensuring all PII has been fully redacted. Then submit. The AI system extracts key clinical data and produces a consolidated timeline, enabling rapid identification of periods of potential patient deterioration.

4. Stark Law Compliance Check

Scenario

A hospital proposes offering financial bonuses to physicians based on the volume of X-rays ordered. Legal counsel must explain why this compensation arrangement violates federal referral restrictions under the Stark Law.

> ***Prompt***
>
> *"Explain the 'Volume or Value of Referrals' prohibition under the Stark Law to a hospital administrator. Use a hypothetical involving diagnostic X-ray referrals to illustrate why compensating physicians based on test volume is prohibited. Maintain an advisory and cautionary tone."*

How It Works

Using an AI tool such as ChatGPT, first enter the prompt and submit. The AI will translate statutory language into clear business guidance, allowing hospital administrators to understand regulatory boundaries and compliance risks without needing technical legal expertise.

5. Food and Drug Administration Regulatory Pathway Summary

Scenario

A biotechnology startup plans to launch a mobile medical application but is uncertain whether the product requires formal oversight by the Food and Drug Administration or qualifies for the "General Wellness" regulatory exemption.

Prompt

"Summarize Food and Drug Administration guidance on Software as a Medical Device. Explain the criteria for the 'General Wellness' policy exemption. Provide a checklist to determine whether a fitness tracking application requires pre-market notification clearance under Section 510(k) or qualifies for exemption."

How It Works

Using research platforms such as Perplexity AI or Gemini, first enter the prompt and submit. The AI retrieves relevant regulatory guidance documents and synthesizes them into a structured decision checklist that assists early-stage regulatory planning and risk assessment.

33

International Law

The Essential Role of the International Lawyer

International lawyers operate across jurisdictions, representing clients in cross-border commercial transactions, international arbitration, treaty-based disputes, and human rights matters. They manage conflicts of laws, treaty interpretation, and culturally diverse legal systems while advising on transactions and disputes that transcend national boundaries.

Common Challenges Faced by International Lawyers

A primary challenge is jurisdictional friction—determining which country's laws and courts govern a dispute. Language barriers, divergent legal traditions, and the complexity of synthesizing international conventions such as the United Nations Convention on Contracts for the International Sale of Goods (CISG) further complicate research, drafting, and negotiation.

How AI Simplifies International Law Tasks

AI functions as a comparative legal analyst. It can rapidly compare statutory regimes across jurisdictions, translate legal concepts as functional equivalents rather than literal terms, and summarize complex treaties or arbitral rules for application to specific fact patterns.

Crafting Effective Prompts for International Law Tasks

This section provides prompts designed for global legal practice. The examples show how AI can assist in determining governing law, drafting international arbitration clauses, preparing functional legal translations, and synthesizing multinational compliance rules to bridge both jurisdictional and linguistic gaps.

1. Legal Contract Translation (French to English)

Scenario

A United Kingdom–based lawyer is reviewing a commercial lease for a client expanding operations into Paris. The lawyer must translate a French force majeure clause into English while accurately expressing civil law concepts such as imprévision that lack direct common law equivalents.

> ***Prompt***
> *"Act as a senior legal translator fluent in French civil law and English common law. Translate the French contract clause below into English using a functional-equivalent approach rather than a word-for-word translation. Capture the intended legal effect for an English-speaking lawyer. After completing the translation, add a 'Translator's Note' explaining any civil-law concepts, including the distinction between force majeure and imprévision, that do not have direct equivalents in common law."*

How It Works

Using ChatGPT, Gemini, or Microsoft Copilot, first enter the prompt, then paste the French contract clause, and submit. The AI generates an English translation drafted in professional legal style and includes explanatory notes identifying legal nuances and potential interpretive risks.

2. Choice of Law and Forum Analysis

Scenario

A German company initiates litigation against a United States supplier. The contract contains no governing law clause. The lawyer must assess which jurisdiction's laws and courts are most likely to assert authority over the dispute.

Prompt

"Act as an expert in international conflict of laws. Analyze a dispute between a German buyer and a U.S. seller where the contract is silent on governing law. Apply the European Union Rome I Regulation and the United States Restatement (Second) of Conflict of Laws to evaluate which jurisdiction's law is likely to govern, focusing on the 'closest connection' test."

How It Works

Using CoCounsel, or ChatGPT, first enter the prompt and submit. The AI compares European and U.S. choice-of-law frameworks and provides a structured assessment of jurisdictional outcomes.

3. International Arbitration Clause Drafting

Scenario

A client is entering into a joint venture with a counterparty based in a jurisdiction with concerns regarding court independence. The lawyer seeks to channel all disputes into neutral international arbitration seated in London.

> ***Prompt***
>
> *"Draft a binding arbitration clause for a cross-border joint venture agreement. Designate the London Court of International Arbitration (LCIA) as the arbitral forum. Specify London as the seat of arbitration, English as the language of proceedings, and a panel of three arbitrators. Include a waiver of sovereign immunity to ensure enforceability."*

How It Works

Using ChatGPT, first enter the prompt and submit. The AI drafts a comprehensive arbitration clause aligned with LCIA model provisions and international enforcement standards.

4. Comparative Law Explanation (Good Faith)

Scenario

A United States lawyer negotiating a contract with a French counterpart encounters repeated references to a statutory "duty of good faith." The lawyer needs to understand how this obligation differs from common law principles.

> ***Prompt***
>
> *"Compare the concept of 'good faith' in commercial contracting under French civil law and New York common law. Explain the practical implications for a U.S. client negotiating with a French counterparty and assess whether French law imposes a stronger duty to negotiate in good faith."*

How It Works

Using Perplexity AI, or ChatGPT, first enter the prompt and submit. The AI provides a comparative doctrinal explanation, highlighting the stricter statutory role of good faith under French law and its negotiation consequences.

5. Sanctions Compliance Check

Scenario

A client plans to export software to a foreign distributor whose subsidiary operates in a sanctioned jurisdiction. The lawyer must determine whether approval of the transaction triggers liability under facilitation rules.

> ***Prompt***
>
> *"Summarize the restrictions under U.S. Office of Foreign Assets Control (OFAC) regulations regarding 'facilitation' of transactions involving sanctioned entities. Specifically explain whether a U.S. parent company may authorize or approve a transaction conducted by a non-U.S. subsidiary involving a blocked jurisdiction."*

How It Works

Using Perplexity AI or Gemini, first enter the prompt and submit. The AI synthesizes sanctions guidance and explains the strict liability risks associated with prohibited facilitation.

34

Sports Law

The Essential Role of the Sports Lawyer

Sports lawyers represent athletes, clubs, leagues, and governing bodies across domestic and international markets. Their work spans high-value player contracts, transfer negotiations, sponsorship and endorsement agreements, and representation in disciplinary proceedings involving misconduct or anti-doping violations. The practice is fast-paced and highly sensitive to media, regulatory deadlines, and reputational risk.

Common Challenges Faced by Sports Lawyers

Sports law operates under intense time pressure, particularly during cross-border transfer windows when transactions must close within hours. Practitioners navigate complex regulatory frameworks, including international federation rules such as FIFA Regulations, collective bargaining agreements, and national labor laws. Protecting athlete image rights has become increasingly complex amid social media monetization, esports licensing, and expanding digital markets.

How AI Simplifies Sports Law Tasks

AI functions as an always-available legal assistant for contract analysis and multilingual review. It rapidly translates and evaluates foreign transfer agreements, audits sponsorship contracts for exclusivity and conflict risks, and summarizes lengthy disciplinary rulings from the Court of Arbitration for Sport (CAS), allowing lawyers to respond at the speed the industry demands.

Crafting Effective Prompts for Sports Law Tasks

This section provides prompts tailored to the high-velocity environment of sports practice. The examples demonstrate how AI can support urgent contract translations, sponsorship exclusivity reviews, drafting of modern image-rights clauses, and disciplinary defense research, equipping lawyers to act decisively under strict deadlines.

1. Player Transfer Agreement Translation (Spanish to English)

Scenario

An English Premier League club is finalizing the signing of a striker from a Spanish La Liga side on Transfer Deadline Day. The Spanish club submits the transfer agreement in Spanish. The UK lawyer requires an immediate translation of the Buy-Out Clause to verify the total fee exposure.

> ***Prompt***
>
> *"Act as a Sports Law specialist fluent in Spanish and English. Translate the following 'Cláusula de Rescisión' (Buy-Out Clause) from a Spanish La Liga player contract into English. Ensure accurate translation of technical football legal terms (including distinctions between 'derechos federativos' and 'derechos económicos'). Flag any language indicating whether the buy-out amount includes VAT or related taxes."*

How It Works

Using ChatGPT or Gemini, first enter the prompt, then paste the Spanish contract clause, and submit. The AI produces a precise legal translation and highlights whether the fee is structured as a net or gross payment.

2. Sponsorship Exclusivity Check

Scenario

An athlete is preparing to sign a sponsorship agreement with Nike. The lawyer must review the athlete's existing endorsement contract with a beverage company to determine whether any exclusivity restrictions apply to apparel or logo placement.

> ***Prompt***
>
> *"Review the 'Exclusivity' and 'Grant of Rights' clauses from the existing sponsorship agreement provided below. Determine whether entering into a new endorsement arrangement with a footwear or athletic-wear brand would constitute a breach. Specifically assess whether the definition of 'Competitor' includes athletic apparel or footwear companies."*

How It Works

Using CoCounsel or ChatGPT, first enter the prompt, then paste the relevant contractual clauses, and submit. The AI analyzes the scope of the non-competition obligations and identifies any potential conflicts that could expose the athlete to breach of contract claims.

3. Image Rights Clause Drafting

Scenario

A professional club seeks to modernize its player contracts to secure rights to exploit player images across emerging digital platforms, including NFTs and metaverse applications. The lawyer must update the standard image rights clause accordingly.

> ***Prompt***
>
> *"Draft a modern 'Group Image Rights' clause for a professional athlete's employment contract. The clause must expressly grant the Club rights to use the Player's name, image, voice, and likeness for digital assets, including NFTs, video games, and metaverse environments. Include provisions addressing usage scope, duration, and revenue-sharing from digital merchandise."*

How It Works

Using ChatGPT, first enter the prompt and submit. The AI generates a forward-looking contractual clause addressing digital rights exploitation and revenue allocation.

4. Disciplinary Defense Strategy (Doping)

Scenario

An athlete records a positive doping test but asserts accidental ingestion through a contaminated supplement. The lawyer must assess recent jurisprudence on the "No Significant Fault or Negligence" defense.

> ***Prompt***
>
> *"Summarize the evidentiary standard for establishing 'No Significant Fault or Negligence' under the World Anti-Doping Code. Provide summaries of three recent Court of Arbitration for Sport (CAS) decisions in which athletes successfully obtained reduced sanctions due to contaminated supplements."*

How It Works

Using Perplexity AI or Clio vLex AI, first enter the prompt and submit. The AI retrieves and summarizes relevant CAS decisions, assisting counsel in developing mitigation arguments.

5. Morality Clause Negotiation

Scenario

A sponsor seeks to terminate an endorsement agreement citing a morality clause after the athlete receives a minor traffic citation. The lawyer must argue that the conduct does not meet the contract's threshold for reputational harm.

> ***Prompt***
>
> *"Act as counsel for the athlete. Review the 'Morality Clause' provided below. Draft a counter-argument letter to the sponsor asserting that the athlete's minor traffic citation does not constitute conduct bringing the brand into 'Public Disrepute' or 'Scandal' under the agreement. Argue that the clause was intended to apply only to serious criminal or materially damaging conduct."*

How It Works

Using ChatGPT, first enter the prompt, then submit. The AI drafts a professional advocacy letter distinguishing minor infractions from contractual grounds for termination.

35

Environmental Law

The Essential Role of the Environmental Lawyer

Environmental lawyers advise on land use approvals, pollution control compliance, hazardous materials regulation, and sustainability obligations. They navigate complex federal, state, and local regulatory frameworks to obtain permits, defend enforcement actions, and manage environmental risk across commercial and industrial operations.

Common Challenges Faced by Environmental Lawyers

This practice area involves extensive technical documentation, including Environmental Impact Statements that may exceed thousands of pages. Lawyers must also track continually evolving emission standards and address "legacy liabilities," involving historic contamination that remains legally actionable during property transactions and corporate acquisitions.

How AI Simplifies Environmental Law Tasks

AI functions as a technical synthesizer. It can summarize lengthy scientific reports into usable executive briefings, monitor regulatory updates, assist in drafting Phase I due diligence inquiry correspondence, and support research and preparation in environmental litigation matters.

Crafting Effective Prompts for Environmental Tasks

This section provides prompt templates tailored to the technical demands of Environmental Law. These examples illustrate how artificial intelligence can be used to synthesize Environmental Impact Statements, generate chemical compliance checklists under federal law, and draft protective clauses for risk allocation in environmentally sensitive transactions.

1. Environmental Impact Statement (EIS) Summary

Scenario

A lawyer is assisting a community group opposing the proposed construction of a manufacturing facility. The attorney needs to quickly locate and summarize sections of a 1,000-page Draft Environmental Impact Statement addressing groundwater contamination risks.

> ***Prompt***
>
> *"You are an Environmental Law Analyst. Review the attached text from the Draft Environmental Impact Statement (EIS). Extract and summarize the findings related to 'Groundwater Resources,' 'Aquifer Contamination Potential,' and 'Water Table Impacts.' Highlight any statements acknowledging 'unavoidable adverse impacts' and cite corresponding page references."*

How It Works

Using CoCounsel or Gemini, first enter the prompt. Next, upload the relevant chapters of the Draft Environmental Impact Statement in word or PDF Format. Then submit. The AI isolates critical scientific findings and highlights regulatory admissions needed for legal analysis and advocacy development.

2. Regulatory Compliance Checklist (Chemicals)

Scenario

A manufacturing client plans to import a new chemical solvent into the United States. The lawyer must identify all reporting and regulatory requirements under the Toxic Substances Control Act prior to market introduction.

Prompt

"Create a compliance checklist for a United States manufacturer importing a new chemical substance under the Toxic Substances Control Act. Include steps covering (1) Pre-Manufacture Notice submission requirements, (2) Inventory verification procedures, and (3) assessment under Significant New Use Rules. Format the output as a step-by-step action plan."

How It Works

Using Perplexity AI or Gemini, first enter the prompt. Then submit. The AI generates a structured compliance checklist outlining required actions and sequencing to help ensure adherence to Environmental Protection Agency reporting obligations.

3. Clause Drafting: Environmental Indemnity

Scenario

A buyer is purchasing a gas station property containing historical underground fuel storage tanks. The lawyer must prepare an indemnity clause protecting the buyer from liability tied to any pre-closing contamination.

> ***Prompt***
>
> *"Draft an 'Environmental Indemnity' clause for a commercial real estate purchase agreement involving a gas station. Require the Seller to indemnify the Buyer against all remediation costs, regulatory fines, penalties, and enforcement actions arising from any pre-closing release of hazardous materials, including contamination associated with Underground Storage Tanks. State that the indemnity shall survive closing indefinitely."*

How It Works

Using Clio vLex or ChatGPT, first enter the prompt. Then submit. The AI drafts a commercially structured indemnity clause allocating environmental risk to the Seller for counsel review and refinement.

4. Case Law Research: Standing to Sue

Scenario

A non-profit organization intends to bring an environmental enforcement action. The lawyer must confirm whether the organization has standing based on injuries to its members.

> ***Prompt***
>
> *"Summarize Federal Court decisions issued within the past five years concerning 'organizational standing' in environmental citizen-suit actions. Focus on cases where non-profit plaintiffs established standing based on injuries to members' recreational, environmental, or health interests. Identify the jurisdiction, factual basis for standing, and the court's reasoning."*

How It Works

Using Lexis+ AI, Clio vLex, or CoCounsel, first enter the prompt. Then submit. The AI retrieves relevant precedents and produces a synthesized research summary suitable for drafting jurisdictional pleadings.

5. Environmental, Social, and Governance Reporting Disclosure

Scenario

A publicly traded logistics company must prepare its annual "Climate Risk" disclosure in compliance with Securities and Exchange Commission reporting standards, while avoiding unsupported "greenwashing" language.

> ***Prompt***
>
> *"Draft a 'Climate Risk Factors' disclosure for a Securities and Exchange Commission Form 10-K filing. The company is a logistics firm exposed to rising fuel costs, supply chain disruption, and increased hurricane frequency. The disclosure must be factual, specific, and limited to material financial risks, avoiding aspirational or promotional language."*

How It Works

Using ChatGPT or CoCounsel, first enter the prompt. Then submit. The AI produces a compliance-oriented risk disclosure draft for attorney review and final inclusion in the regulatory filing.

36

Cannabis Law

The Essential Role of the Cannabis Lawyer

Cannabis lawyers provide legal guidance within an evolving regulatory landscape. Their work includes licensing applications, regulatory compliance, business formation, and advising on domestic and international trade in medical cannabis. They counsel clients across all stages of the value chain—including cultivation, processing, distribution, retail sales, and consumption—and resolve disputes arising in this highly regulated industry.

Common Challenges Faced by Cannabis Lawyers

The cannabis legal environment is defined by regulatory fragmentation and inconsistency. Lawyers must reconcile state-level legalization frameworks with continued federal or international prohibitions. Rapid regulatory changes, shifting compliance standards, evolving tax rules, zoning restrictions, and persistent public stigma create ongoing legal and business risks for clients. Maintaining up-to-date regulatory knowledge across multiple jurisdictions remains one of the profession's greatest challenges.

How AI Simplifies Cannabis Law Tasks

AI functions as an advanced regulatory research and documentation assistant. AI tools can:Track and compare state licensing requirements, Draft Standard Operating Procedures (SOPs) for regulatory submissions, and Review product labeling and packaging for compliance with safety and advertising regulations.

Crafting Effective Prompts for Cannabis Tasks

This section provides practical prompts for navigating the complex regulatory frameworks governing cannabis. The examples address common legal challenges—ranging from state social equity licensing assessments to international compliance documentation—and demonstrate how AI can support lawyers working within jurisdictions affected by regulatory divergence and cross-border restrictions.

1. State Licensing Comparison

Scenario

A client operates a dispensary in Colorado and wants to expand to New York. The lawyer needs to explain the key differences in "Social Equity" licensing requirements between the two states.

> ***Prompt***
>
> *"Compare the 'Social Equity' cannabis licensing requirements in New York (Marijuana Regulation and Taxation Act) versus Colorado. Create a comparison table addressing: (1) Eligibility criteria for applicants, (2) Fee waivers or grants available, and (3) Priority review status. Focus on implications for a minority-owned business."*

How It Works

Using Perplexity AI or Gemini, first, enter the prompt. Then, submit. The AI synthesizes current regulatory guidance and statutory frameworks from both jurisdictions, producing a comparative overview that supports feasibility analysis for business expansion.

2. Legal Analysis of Cannabis Possession and Arrest

Scenario

A client has been arrested for cannabis possession in a state where medical marijuana use is legal but recreational use remains prohibited. The lawyer must evaluate the legality of the charges.

Prompt

"Review the provided arrest record, police report, and medical marijuana identification card for a client arrested for cannabis possession. Analyze whether the charges comply with state medical cannabis laws and identify potential defenses, including valid medical authorization or improper law enforcement application of statutes."

How It Works

Using ChatGPT or Gemini, first, enter the prompt. Next, upload the arrest record, police report, and medical marijuana ID. Then, submit. After reviewing the uploaded documentation, the AI evaluates statutory requirements for lawful possession and flags possible procedural or evidentiary defenses.

3. EU-GMP Standard Operating Procedure (SOP)

Scenario

A cannabis cultivator plans to export medical cannabis to the European Union and must ensure its drying process complies with EU Good Manufacturing Practice standards. The lawyer must draft a compliant SOP framework.

> ***Prompt***
>
> *"Draft a Standard Operating Procedure (SOP) structure for 'Batch Release and Certification' of medical cannabis flower, compliant with EU-GMP (EudraLex Volume 4). Include sections for: (1) Quality Person review procedures , (2) Testing for heavy metals and pesticides, and (3) Certificate of Analysis verification processes."*

How It Works

Using ChatGPT, first, enter the prompt. Then, submit. The AI produces an audit-ready SOP framework aligned with European pharmaceutical inspection standards.

4. Packaging Compliance Review

Scenario

A client has developed packaging for a cannabis gummy product and requires an assessment of compliance concerning state prohibitions against marketing that "appeals to children."

> ***Prompt***
>
> *"Review the description of the proposed cannabis edible packaging provided below. Analyze its compliance with [Insert State] regulations regarding marketing and labeling restrictions related to appeal to children. Identify specific violations and recommend compliant packaging modifications."*

How It Works

Using ChatGPT or Gemini, first, enter the prompt. Next, upload the packaging descriptions, then, submit. The AI compares packaging elements such as imagery, color usage, typography, and product resemblance to confectionery against applicable regulations to identify compliance risks and provide corrective guidance.

5. Supply Agreement (Quality Warranties)

Scenario

A distributor is purchasing bulk cannabis oil for international export. The receiving jurisdiction imposes strict THC limits (e.g., below 0.2% or 1.0%, depending on the country).

> ***Prompt***
>
> *Draft a 'Product Quality and Regulatory Compliance' warranty clause for an International Cannabis Supply Agreement. The Supplier must warrant that all products meet the legally required THC thresholds of the Destination Jurisdiction as defined in the schedule. Include indemnification provisions for losses arising from customs seizure or destruction caused by non-compliant THC concentrations."*

How It Works

Using ChatGPT, first, enter the prompt. Then, submit. The AI drafts a commercial warranty clause allocating regulatory risk to the supplier in cases of non-compliant shipments.

37

AI & Data Privacy Law

The Essential Role of the AI & Privacy Lawyer

AI and data privacy law is now a truly global practice. Lawyers in this field manage the legal risks of processing personal data and deploying AI systems across jurisdictions. They advise on compliance with regulations such as the European Union General Data Protection Regulation (GDPR), California Consumer Privacy Act (CCPA), Brazil's LGPD, South Africa's POPIA, and emerging AI-specific laws like the EU AI Act. Their work includes drafting Data Processing Agreements (DPAs), performing Data Protection Impact Assessments (DPIAs), and monitoring cross-border AI deployments for regulatory conformity.

Common Challenges Faced by Privacy Lawyers

The landscape is fragmented and rapidly evolving. Practitioners must navigate multiple national and regional frameworks, translating technical architectures—APIs, machine learning models, and data pipelines—into legally compliant practices. Lawyers also face challenges with algorithmic risk assessments, international data transfers, AI transparency obligations, and conducting DPIAs for novel AI applications that may not yet be explicitly regulated.

How AI Simplifies Privacy Tasks

AI tools accelerate compliance and risk analysis worldwide. They can generate the first draft of a DPIA for high-risk AI systems, scan contracts for missing data-protection clauses, classify cookies and trackers for consent management, and synthesize cross-jurisdictional privacy obligations. By automating labor-intensive processes, AI allows lawyers to focus on nuanced legal reasoning, ethical assessments, and strategic risk management.

Crafting Effective Prompts for AI & Privacy Tasks

This section illustrates how AI can support global privacy compliance. Prompts are designed to manage cross-border governance, evaluate AI risk, and draft standardized agreements under multiple legal regimes.

1. Data Protection Impact Assessment (DPIA) Generator

Scenario

A multinational company is deploying a facial recognition system for office access in the EU, UK, and Brazil. The lawyer must draft a DPIA covering GDPR, UK Data Protection Act 2018, and LGPD requirements.

> ***Prompt***
>
> *"Act as a Privacy Counsel. Draft a 'Data Protection Impact Assessment' (DPIA) for a biometric facial recognition system used for employee access. Cover: (1) Purpose of processing, (2) Necessity and proportionality across jurisdictions, (3) Risks to data subjects' rights under GDPR, LGPD, and UK Data Protection Act, and (4) Proposed mitigation measures including encryption, retention limits, and access controls."*

How It Works

Using ChatGPT or Gemini, first enter the prompt, then submit. The AI generates a structured DPIA addressing multinational compliance obligations.

2. AI Acceptable Use Policy

Scenario

Employees in offices across multiple countries are using generative AI tools. The General Counsel requires a global policy to manage AI usage while remaining compliant with local laws.

> ***Prompt***
>
> *"Draft a 'Generative AI Acceptable Use Policy' for a multinational workforce. Permit AI for ideation and drafting, but prohibit: (1) Inputting personal or sensitive data without consent, (2) Using AI outputs without human verification, and (3) Deploying AI in ways that violate GDPR, CCPA, LGPD, or other local data-protection laws. Include mandatory disclosure requirements."*

How It Works

Using ChatGPT, first enter the prompt, then submit. The AI drafts a policy that balances innovation and global risk management.

3. Vendor Data Processing Agreement (DPA) Review

Scenario

A company engages a cloud provider in multiple regions. The lawyer needs to ensure the contract includes mandatory data-protection clauses under GDPR, CCPA, and other applicable laws.

> ***Prompt***
>
> *"Review the vendor agreement provided. Check for required Data Processing clauses under GDPR Article 28, CCPA obligations, and relevant local regulations. Highlight missing clauses and draft compliant text where necessary."*

How It Works

Using Lexis+ AI or ChatGPT, first, enter the prompt. Next, paste the contract text below it, then submit. The AI identifies gaps and drafts missing clauses to mitigate international compliance risk.

Copyrighted Material

4. Cross-Border Data Breach Notification Timeline

Scenario

A company experiences a cyberattack affecting users in the EU, UK, Brazil, and California. The lawyer needs a global notification plan.

> ***Prompt***
>
> *"Create a 'Data Breach Notification Timeline' for affected jurisdictions including EU, UK, Brazil, and California. List reporting deadlines, responsible authorities, triggers for notification, and required content under each law."*

How It Works

Using Perplexity AI or Gemini, first enter the prompt, then submit. The AI produces a structured timeline detailing regulatory obligations across multiple countries.

5. Cookie and Tracking Classification

Scenario

A global e-commerce site collects cookies in the EU, UK, and Brazil. The lawyer must classify trackers to ensure consent compliance under regional privacy laws.

> ***Prompt***
>
> *"Classify cookies and tracking technologies into 'Strictly Necessary,' 'Performance,' and 'Targeting/Advertising.' Indicate which require opt-in consent under GDPR, UK Data Protection Act, and LGPD. Explain legal reasoning for each category."*

How It Works

Using ChatGPT, first enter the prompt, then submit. The AI categorizes cookies for consent management and global compliance guidance.

Conclusion

The Future of Legal Practice

The legal profession has long defined itself by its stewardship of precedent—the disciplined application of accumulated wisdom to contemporary disputes. Throughout this guide, we have shown that Artificial Intelligence does not interrupt this tradition; rather, it enhances and accelerates it.

Across the Prompt Packs in Part VI, it becomes clear that AI is remarkably adaptive. It can serve as a tireless researcher for the litigator, a meticulous drafter for the corporate attorney, a pattern analyst for the IP practitioner, or a clear communicator for the immigration lawyer. In every domain—from Employment Law to Cannabis Law—AI reduces administrative friction, refines complex analysis, and expands a lawyer's capacity to focus on the tasks that remain distinctly human: strategic judgment, ethical discernment, and empathetic engagement.

The New Standard of Competence

As we conclude, one truth stands unambiguously before the profession: the question is no longer *whether* lawyers should use AI, but *how* they must use it to remain competent, compliant, and competitive. The "AI-Augmented Lawyer" is not an abstract ideal. It is the new baseline—a professional standard emerging across jurisdictions and practice areas.

Those who develop the capabilities outlined in this book—Prompt Engineering, Hallucination Verification, Model Selection, and Ethical Deployment—will gain a measurable competitive advantage. They will deliver work of higher quality, at unprecedented speed, while maintaining the accuracy and professional rigor that clients and courts demand.

A Final Charge

Yet this transformation carries profound responsibility. The speed and power of AI must never outrun the integrity of legal practice. As you weave these tools into your daily workflow, remember that AI is the engine—but *you* are the steering wheel. Your professional judgment, not the model's output, determines the fairness, accuracy, and justice of the final deliverable.

You now possess the full toolkit.
You have the frameworks, the safeguards, and the prompts.
The future of your practice is yours to shape.
The next chapter of legal innovation is waiting—
and it begins with your next prompt.

Bibliography

Bibliography

Nils J. Nilsson, (2010).The quest for artificial intelligence : a history of ideas and achievements. Cambridge University Press.

McCarthy, J., Minsky, M. L., Rochester, N., & Shannon, C. E. (1955). *A Proposal for the Dartmouth Summer Research Project on Artificial Intelligence.*

Russell, S., & Norvig, P. (2021). *Artificial Intelligence: A Modern Approach* (4th ed.). Pearson Education.

Surden, H. (2019). *Artificial Intelligence and Law: An Overview. Georgia State University Law Review*, 35(4), 1305–1322.

Ashley, K. D. (2017). *Artificial Intelligence and Legal Analytics: New Tools for Law Practice in the Digital Age*. Cambridge University Press.

Katz, D. M., Bommarito, M. J., & Blackman, J. (2017). *A General Approach for Predicting the Behavior of the Supreme Court of the United States. PLOS ONE*, 12(4), e0174698.

Vogl, R., Casanovas, P., & Engemann, C. (2020). *Natural Language Processing in Legal Tech. Artificial Intelligence and Law*, 28(2), 133–159.

Li, Y., & Hu, J. (2022). *Computer Vision in Legal Evidence Analysis. Journal of Law, Technology and Policy*, 2022(1), 56–74.

Ransbotham, S., & Kiron, D. (2020). *The Robotics Transformation of Professional Services. MIT Sloan Management Review*, 62(1), 1–10.

Gardner, A. (1987). *An Artificial Intelligence Approach to Legal Reasoning*. MIT Press.

Susskind, R. (2023). *Tomorrow's Lawyers: An Introduction to Your Future* (3rd ed.). Oxford University Press.

Kaplan, J., & Haenlein, M. (2020). *Rulers of the World, Unite! The Challenges and Opportunities of Artificial Intelligence. Business Horizons, 63*(1), 37–50.

McGinnis, J. O., & Pearce, R. G. (2014). *The Great Disruption: How Machine Intelligence Will Transform the Role of Lawyers in the Delivery of Legal Services. Fordham Law Review, 82*(6), 3041–3066.

Surden, H. (2019). *Artificial Intelligence and Law: An Overview. Georgia State University Law Review, 35*(4), 1305–1337.

Deloitte. (2022). *The Future of Legal Services: AI and Automation*. Deloitte Insights Report.

OECD. (2023). *Artificial Intelligence in the Legal Sector: Efficiency, Ethics, and Regulation*. OECD Digital Economy Papers.

Westlaw Edge. (2023). *AI-Powered Legal Research and Insights*. Thomson Reuters White Paper.

OpenAI. (2024). *Applications of GPT Models in Legal Research and Drafting*. OpenAI Technical Brief.

Katz, D. M., Bommarito, M. J., & Blackman, J. (2017). *A General Approach for Predicting the Behavior of the Supreme Court of the United States. PLOS ONE, 12*(4), e0174698.

Remus, D., & Levy, F. (2016). *Can Robots Be Lawyers? Computers, Lawyers, and the Practice of Law. SSRN Electronic Journal.*

PwC. (2023). *AI and Predictive Analytics in Legal Compliance and Risk Management*. PwC Insights Report.

Accenture. (2022). *Legal Service Delivery in the Age of AI: Enhancing the Client Journey*. Accenture Legal Tech Review.

IBM Legal Tech Division. (2023). *AI and Client-Centric Law Practice: Applications and Outcomes*. IBM White Paper.

American Bar Association (ABA). (2024). *AI in Legal Education: Integrating Technology into Law Curricula*. ABA Education Series.

Stanford Law School. (2023). *AI Tools in Legal Training and Practice Readiness*. Stanford Legal AI Lab Report.

Harvard Law Review. (2024). *AI-Driven Legal Education: Pedagogical Opportunities and Ethical Challenges*. *Harvard Law Review, 137*(2), 312–339.

OECD. (2019). *OECD principles on artificial intelligence*. Organisation for Economic Co- operation and Development. https://www.oecd.org/en/topics/sub-issues/ai-principles.html

UNESCO. (2021). *Recommendation on the ethics of artificial intelligence*. United Nations Educational, Scientific and Cultural Organization. https://unesdoc.unesco.org/ark:/48223/pf0000373434

European Commission. (2021). *Proposal for an artificial intelligence act*. Brussels: European Commission. https://digital-strategy.ec.europa.eu/en/library/proposal-artificial-intelligence-act

European Union. (2016). *General Data Protection Regulation (GDPR)*. Official Journal of the European Union. https://eur-lex.europa.eu/legal-content/EN/TXT/?uri=CELEX%3A32016R0679

GDPR: Regulation (EU) 2016/679 (General Data Protection Regulation), Art. 22 (Automated individual decision-making, including profiling).

U.S. Congress. (2019). *Algorithmic Accountability Act*. Washington, DC: United States Congress. https://www.congress.gov/bill/116th-congress/house-bill/2231

Federal Guidance: National Institute of Standards and Technology (NIST). *Artificial Intelligence Risk Management Framework (AI RMF 1.0)*, NIST AI 100-1 (Jan. 2023).

National Institute of Standards and Technology (NIST). (2023). *Artificial Intelligence Risk Management Framework (AI RMF 1.0)*. U.S. Department of Commerce. https://nvlpubs.nist.gov/nistpubs/ai/nist.ai.100-1.pdf

Executive Order: Exec. Order No. 14,179, *Reducing Barriers to Artificial Intelligence Innovation* (Jan. 2025). *(Note: Cited as per text; refer also to Exec. Order 14,110 (2023) for foundational safety standards).*

State of California. (2018). *California Consumer Privacy Act (CCPA)*. California Legislature. https://oag.ca.gov/privacy/ccpa

State of California. (2020). *California Privacy Rights Act (CPRA)*. California Legislature. https://www.caprivacy.org/cpra/

U.S. Congress. (1998). *Children's Online Privacy Protection Act (COPPA)*. Washington, DC: United States Congress. https://www.ftc.gov/legal-library/browse/rules/childrens-online-privacy-protection-rule-coppa

Government of Canada. (2019). *Directive on automated decision-making*. Treasury Board of Canada Secretariat. https://www.canada.ca/en/government/system/digital-government/digital-government-innovations/automated-decision-making.html

Government of Canada. (2022). *Artificial Intelligence and Data Act (AIDA), Bill C-27*. Parliament of Canada. https://www.parl.ca/DocumentViewer/en/44-1/bill/C-27/first-reading

Australian Government. (2019). *AI ethics framework*. Department of Industry, Science and Resources. https://www.industry.gov.au/publications/australias-ai-ethics-framework

Personal Data Protection Commission (Singapore). (2022). *Model AI governance framework (updated)*. Singapore: PDPC. https://www.pdpc.gov.sg/

Government of Japan. (2022). *AI governance guidelines*. Tokyo: Council for Science, Technology and Innovation. https://www8.cao.go.jp/cstp/english/ai/ai_guidelines.html

Argentina (AI)Consejo de la Magistratura. (2024). *Programa Nacional de Inteligencia Artificial en la Justicia (Resolución 111/2024)*. Boletín Oficial.

Brazil: *Projeto de Lei n° 2338, de 2023* (Legal Framework for Artificial Intelligence). Senate of Brazil.

United Arab Emirates Government. (2021). *Federal Decree-Law No. 45 of 2021 Regarding the Protection of Personal Data.* Official

State of Qatar. (2016). *Law No. 13 of 2016 on Protecting Personal Data Privacy.* Al Meezan.

Continental Strategy: African Union. *Continental Strategy on Artificial Intelligence.* AU Executive Council, 45th Ordinary Session (Accra, July 2024).

Arab Republic of Egypt. (2020). *Personal Data Protection Law (Law No. 151 of 2020).* Official Gazette.

Nigeria: *Nigeria Data Protection Act, 2023* (Act No. 48 of 2023)

South Africa: *Protection of Personal Information Act* (POPIA), Act No. 4 of 2013, § 71 (Automated Decision Making).

OpenAI. (2025). *ChatGPT Overview*. OpenAI Documentation.

OpenAI. (2024). *Introducing GPT-4 Technical Report.*

Google DeepMind. (2024). *Gemini Model Overview.*

Microsoft. (2024). *Microsoft Copilot for Microsoft 365.*

Perplexity AI. (2025). *Perplexity AI Platform Guide.*

Casetext. (2024). *Introducing CoCounsel: The AI Legal Assistant.*

Harvey AI. (2025). *Harvey AI for Legal Professionals.*

LexisNexis. (2024). *Lexis+ AI Launch and Product Overview.*

American Bar Association. (2023). *Model Rules of Professional Conduct: Rule 1.1 – Competence (Technological Proficiency)*. ABA Publications.

Susskind, R. (2023). *The Future of the Professions: How Technology Will Transform the Work of Human Experts* (3rd ed.). Oxford University Press.

LexisNexis. (2023). *AI and Project Management in Law Firms: The New Paradigm of Efficiency*. LexisNexis Legal Insights.

Deloitte. (2022). *Legal Operations Transformation: Project Management and AI Integration*. Deloitte Legal Operations Series.

Thomson Reuters. (2023). *Legal Project Management: Leveraging AI for Predictability and Efficiency*. Thomson Reuters Legal Intelligence.

Gartner. (2024). *AI-Powered Legal Operations: Workflow Automation and Predictive Management*. Gartner Legal Research.

PwC. (2023). *AI in Legal Services: Managing Resources and Budget with Predictive Analytics*. PwC Legal Research Division.

Lexis+. (2024). *Integrating Financial Forecasting in Legal Practice through AI Systems*. LexisNexis White Paper.

Microsoft. (2024). *Copilot for Microsoft 365 in Legal Teams: Enhancing Productivity through Data Insights*. Microsoft Legal Tech Division.

Casetext. (2024). *AI CoCounsel for Workflow Optimization and Predictive Oversight*. Casetext Legal Innovation Series.

Accenture. (2023). *Strategic Integration of AI in Legal Project Management Frameworks*. Accenture Legal Transformation Studies.

OpenAI. (2024). *ChatGPT Enterprise Capabilities for Legal Teams*. OpenAI Enterprise Division.

Harvey AI. (2024). *Optimizing Legal Workflow Integration through Intelligent Project Management*. Harvey AI Legal Insights.

ABA. (2023). *Guidelines for Ethical AI Use in Law Firms*. American Bar Association Journal of Ethics.

ABA. (2023). *Technological Competence and the Duty of Supervision in the AI Era*. ABA Professional Responsibility Division.

Gartner. (2024). *AI Governance and Data Privacy in Legal Operations*. Gartner Legal Research.

American Bar Association. (2023). *Ethical use of artificial intelligence in legal practice*. ABA Center for Professional Responsibility.

International Legal Technology Association (ILTA). (2024). *LegalTech adoption and evaluation framework*.

Thomson Reuters. (2024). *AI in law: Responsible deployment and governance*.

Gartner, Inc. (2024). *Evaluating enterprise AI for legal workflows: Market guide*.

LexisNexis. (2024). *Lexis+ AI: Product overview and legal research capabilities*.

OpenAI. (2025). *ChatGPT and ChatGPT Enterprise: Use cases for professional workflows*.

Harvey AI. (2024). *Harvey for law firms: Enterprise legal AI platform overview*.

Perplexity Labs. (2025). *Perplexity Pro: Research, verification, and citation features*.

Microsoft. (2025). *Microsoft 365 Copilot: Product documentation and legal scenarios*.

Google DeepMind. (2025). *Gemini: Multimodal models and enterprise applications*.

Casetext. (2024). *Introducing CoCounsel: An AI assistant for attorneys*.

Ashley, Kevin D. Artificial Intelligence and Legal Reasoning. Cambridge, MA: MIT Press, 2017. (A foundational text on AI and law)

Bick, Lilian, and Mireille Hildebrandt. "Algorithmic Regulation: Bridging Law and Computer Science." Computer Law & Security Review 33, no. 6 (2017): 869-883. (Discusses the challenges of regulating AI)

Danaher, John. "The Limits of Algorithmic Law." Harvard Journal of Law & Technology 31, no. 1 (2017): 1-66. (Explores the limitations of using algorithms in law)

Hildebrandt, Mireille. Law, Governance, and the Algorithm: On the Regulation of Automated Decision-Making. Oxford: Oxford University Press, 2018. (Discusses the legal and ethical implications of automated decision-making)

O'Neil, Cathy. Weapons of Math Destruction: How Big Data Increases Inequality and Threatens Democracy. New York: Crown, 2016. (While not specifically about law, this book is highly relevant to the biases inherent in algorithms)

Pasquale, Frank. The Black Box Society: The Secret Algorithms That Control Money and Information. Cambridge, MA: Harvard University Press,1 2015. (Explores the lack of transparency in algorithmic decision-making)

Barfield, W., & Pagallo, U. (2023). *Research handbook on the law of artificial intelligence*. Edward Elgar Publishing.

European Commission. (2024). *AI Act and ethical AI guidelines for fairness and transparency*. Retrieved from https://digital-strategy.ec.europa.eu

Mittelstadt, B., Russell, C., & Wachter, S. (2023). *Explaining explanations in AI*. Journal of Artificial Intelligence Research, 78(2), 121–149.

Floridi, L., & Cowls, J. (2022). *A unified framework of five principles for AI in society*. Harvard Data Science Review, 4(1).

European Union. (2024). *General Data Protection Regulation (GDPR) and right to explanation*. Official Journal of the European Union.

UNESCO. (2023). *Recommendation on the ethics of artificial intelligence*. UNESCO Digital Library.

About the Author

Eric Agyemang Duah is a Generative AI specialist, author, and consultant whose work focuses on the responsible, practical, and profession-specific application of Artificial Intelligence systems. His research and advisory practice examine how AI can be integrated into established professional workflows, particularly in law, education, and other knowledge-driven fields, while upholding ethical standards, regulatory awareness, and professional accountability.

Eric specializes in Generative AI training, AI reliability assessment, and the mitigation of ethical and operational risks associated with AI-assisted decision-making. He is widely recognized for translating complex AI technologies into structured, actionable frameworks that enable institutions and professionals without technical backgrounds to adopt AI effectively and responsibly. His work bridges emerging AI capabilities with disciplined professional judgment, positioning AI as an augmentative tool rather than a substitute for human expertise.

Connect with Eric on LinkedIn at **linkedin.com/in/prompttech**.

Index

A

www.ingramcontent.com/pod-product-compliance
Lightning Source LLC
LaVergne TN
LVHW080039210926
848481LV00011B/3233
* 9 7 9 8 2 3 0 7 1 4 6 1 3 *